William M. F. Petrie

Religion and Conscience in Ancient Egypt

Lectures delivered at University College in London

William M. F. Petrie

Religion and Conscience in Ancient Egypt
Lectures delivered at University College in London

ISBN/EAN: 9783337236090

Printed in Europe, USA, Canada, Australia, Japan

Cover: Foto ©Lupo / pixelio.de

More available books at **www.hansebooks.com**

RELIGION AND CONSCIENCE IN ANCIENT EGYPT

LECTURES DELIVERED AT
UNIVERSITY COLLEGE, LONDON

BY

W. M. FLINDERS PETRIE

D.C.L., LL.D., Ph.D.

NEW YORK:
CHARLES SCRIBNER'S SONS
153-157 FIFTH AVENUE
1898

PREFACE

THESE lectures, though based on the literature of the Egyptians, cover also some general considerations which are equally applicable to the Religion and Conscience of other nations. They are intended as an attempt to indicate lines of study, and to observe what actually is the construction of human thought, as shown in some of the oldest and most continuous records. It may be said that the relation of these to certain standard views in ethics and religion should have been treated; and that some more logical and systematic ideas are needed to start from. But my object was to see what really is, and not to try to fit that in with any theories, however highly supported, or any views, however orthodox. Treating the divagations of human thought as if they must have been systematic and logical has been the bane of all theories; and many a house of cards has been built to match one single fact or principle which has been grasped. I do not touch the larger questions here, but only deal with what we can readily see and prove; and in this place I no more attempt to enquire what lies behind the growth of ideas here traced, than the biologist enquires what lies behind the comparison and nature of the structures which he unravels. We each try to see what actually exists; usually a safe and needful course before attempting to account for its results or its causes.

I need hardly say that these are mere sketches, intended to suggest a mode of looking at the subject; and any one who might expect from the title to find a full account of matters so vast and complex, will be disarmed when he sees what a mere note-book this volume is.

The Religion lectures are arranged as first used; but the Conscience lectures seemed better to be here re-arranged into three, rather than two as originally delivered. The final notes deal with matters too lengthy for the scale of the lectures.

CONTENTS

	PAGE
PREFACE	5

LECTURE I.
THE HISTORICAL CONDITIONS OF RELIGIONS

1. The need of realizing other minds	11
2. What is religion?	13
3. The origin of intolerance	16
4. Intolerance adopted religion	19
5. Mixed religions of mixed races	20
6. Law of mixture of religions	23
7. Mixture in Egypt	26

LECTURE II.
THE POPULAR RELIGION OF EGYPT

8. Magic in the tales	28
9. Nature of the soul, *Ba* and *Ka*	30
10. The tree spirit	33
11. The sacred animals	36
12. The Fates	38
13. The nature of the gods	39
14. Objects of piety	43
15. Isis and Horus worship of late times	45

LECTURE III.
THE DISCORDANCES OF EGYPTIAN RELIGION

16. Earthly theory of the soul	48
17. Elysian and Solar theories	50

CONTENTS

	PAGE
18. Mummifying theory	51
19. Varying beliefs about gods	52
20. Due to differences of race	54
21. The Set and Horus discordance	56
22. The superfluity of Hathor	58
23. The discordance of Sebek	62
24. Multiplicity of gods of one function	63

LECTURE IV.

ANALYSIS OF THE EGYPTIAN MYTHOLOGY

25. General review of the divinities	68
26. Spirits	70
27. Animals	71
28. Local and minor deities	73
29. Groups of the great gods	74
30. Animal gods	76
31. Human gods	76
32. Cosmic gods	79
33. Abstract gods	81
34. Foreign gods	83
35. Fluctuations of popularity	84

LECTURE V.

THE NATURE OF CONSCIENCE

36. Material for Egyptian study	86
37. The inheritance of conscience	87
38. Intuitions weeded out by utility	90
39. The value of inherited intuitions	93
40. Use of a scale of conscience	95
41. Curve of frequency of varieties	97
42. Conscience money illustrates the law of distribution	101
43. Curves of various types of conscience	104
44. Effect of standards on the conscience	106

CONTENTS

LECTURE VI.

THE INNER DUTIES

	PAGE
45. Classification of duties	110
46. The early lists of duties	111

(1) PERSONAL CHARACTER

47. Character in action	112
48. Character in reserve	116
49. Avoidance of asceticism	120
50. Summary of personal character	121

(2) MATERIAL INTERESTS

51. Material welfare	123
52. Summary of material character	129

(3) FAMILY DUTIES

53. Duties to women	131
54. Duties of parents and children	135

LECTURE VII.

THE OUTER DUTIES

(4) RELATIONS TO EQUALS

55. Honesty and truth	139
56. Kindness	140
57. Public affairs	143

(5) RELATIONS TO SUPERIORS

58. Respect and submission	146
59. In business	150

(6) RELATIONS TO INFERIORS

60. Morally	152
61. Materially	154

(7) DUTIES TO THE GODS

62. In respect	157
63. In propitiation	159
64. Summary of Egyptian character	160

CONTENTS

Note A.
Inherited Intuitions 167

Note B.
The Ideal of Truth, Lucian 169

Note C.
Statistics of Conscience Money . . . 170

Note D.
Nature of the *Ka* . . . 178

ABBREVIATIONS
M. E. E. Maspero, *Études de Mythologie et d'Archéologie Egyptienne*, part ii.
M. H. A. Maspero, *Histoire Ancienne*, tom. i., 1894.
M. Dend. Mariette, *Denderah texte*.
Rec. *Recueil Egyptien* (Maspero).

RELIGION AND CONSCIENCE IN ANCIENT EGYPT

LECTURE I.

THE HISTORICAL CONDITIONS OF RELIGIONS

1. BEFORE considering the Egyptian religion, it will be desirable to look briefly at the general laws which belong to similar cases of a mixture of religions and of races, and to observe what is to be looked for in examining this case in particular. It may seem strange to say that we are greatly in the dark about a religion which has left us the most ample remains of any in the ancient world; but in this case we have enough material to begin to estimate our own ignorance and to realize how much is required before we can understand the mind of another race. That we have in

Egypt to deal with a continuous record of four thousand years before Christianity, and an unknown age before that record, makes our difficulties the greater, but affords us an unparalleled spectacle of religious history and development. And that we have in Egypt to deal with at least four distinguishable races in the earliest history, and a dozen subsequent mixtures of race during recorded history, again makes our difficulties the greater, but gives a fuller example of such a history of a religion than can be found elsewhere.

Before we try to understand another mind—and without such understanding we can never realize another religion—we must quit our present point of view; we must try to see how very different the minds of most other peoples have been from our own at present. We must feel that the greater part of mankind has had systems of language which would be wholly incapable of expressing our ideas; systems of religion which would be a horror to us; ideas of gods which would be monstrous to us; their ways of life would make them flee into the fields from our dwellings; their systems of propriety would bring them into the police court; and their systems of morality would land them at once in the law court. We must set aside all the framework of mind and thought and habit in which we have been formed, and try to leave our ideas free to re-crystallize in a different system. Of course we cannot do all this, we cannot do a tenth of it; but if we can do a very little we shall at least feel how different the world must look, how different the motives must be, among people of another race, another faith, another standard, and another order of things. Close practical contact with a very different race is the best guide to seeing how far apart the organizations of thought are on different bases. Learn to respect, and love, and be intimate with, a man of a far distant stage of life, and you see then how very deep down is the wide platform of elemental feeling and thought which you have together in common; and you begin to perceive how much you have each built on that platform, which isolates you from one another, and makes the point of view of each incomprehensible to the other.

2. In dealing with religion the first question is, What is religion? To say it is the

ideas about a divinity is to limit it at once to theology, which is only a branch of it. And what is a divinity? If it be anything that is worshipped, we are left at once with every visible object included, as there is perhaps no thing or no being that has not been worshipped at some time. The only view which will cover the extremely various instances is that religion is belief concerning any ideas which cannot be immediately verified by the physical senses. The ideas themselves do not constitute religion; but *the act of belief in what is not provable to the senses* is the very basis and limiting boundary of all religions.

The idea of animism which constitutes so large a part of most religions is expressly an explanation of phenomena by bringing in a belief in that which is unprovable. The ideas of primitive medicine, which are incorporated so strongly in savage religion, again are based on beliefs about the unprovable; and as the limits of proof expand by real knowledge, so the limits of religion in medicine contract.

That the idea of personal morality is not an integral part of most religions, is obvious to anyone who has had a practical view of them. Right and wrong do not enter into the circle of religious ideas to most races. The piety of the Carthaginian before Moloch, of the Roman as he sent his captives from the Capitol to be slaughtered in the Colosseum, of Louis XI. as he confided his duplicities to the Virgins in his hat-band, or of Louis XV. as he prayed in the *Parc-aux-Cerfs*, show what the brigand who pays for his masses, or the Arab who swindles in the intervals of his prayers, prove in the present day—that the firmest religious beliefs have no necessary connection with the idea of moral action. In these instances, be it observed, we are not concerned with differences between profession and practice, but with simultaneous acts of the same mind; deeply religious on one side, but destitute of any sense of incongruity between the religion and the action which is recognizedly wrong on the other side. Another principle of many, perhaps most religions, is that they are public and not private; they are collective and not individual. They are concerned with ceremonies, with common action, with the relation of man to man; the initiation, the witch doctor, the tabu, are their prominent parts. The ideal of a purely personal religion, irrespective of any other human being, and inextricably interwoven with the highest sense of right and wrong, is wholly different from what we have to review in the great mass of mankind, and is a growth of which the beginning may be seen but very rarely in ancient times. With that, therefore, we are not concerned at present.

We may then begin to realize how hopeless it is for us to understand the ideas or feelings of those ancient people whose religion we would consider, if we try to interpret their views by our own; or for us to study them without emptying our minds as completely as we can to begin with.

3. One common feature of many religions is intolerance; and it is so essential to realize what this means, that we should look at it closely, the more so as we especially profess in the present time that we have rid ourselves of it, and look on it as being outside of our present motives. Intolerance is one of the strongest instincts of man; it will entirely override his material interests, it can compete with his

strongest passions, and it moulds his social organization. And for what? For merely a question of whether two persons think alike about what cannot be demonstrated to the senses, and what cannot visibly influence their condition in any way. Assuredly no such potent instinct can ever have arisen on such a shadowy ground.

The practical working of intolerance is that it makes a sharp demarcation between one group of men and another; in short, it defines the community, and prevents any person drifting from one community into another without taking a decisive step. It may be said that this only refers to religious communities; but when we look at almost any country or any age but our own, we see that the religious and political communities are coterminous. There is perhaps not an instance to be found of warfare between those who hold exactly the same religious opinions. The Civil War in England was between Church and Nonconformity, the revolution in France was between a Church and Atheism, just as the earlier civil wars had been between Catholicism and Protestantism. The civil and religious communities are identical wherever intolerance has a hold; religion defines the community, and intolerance preserves the boundary.

When we come to consider how far back this state of things has existed we reach an absolute limit for the action of religion at a point when man was incapable of expressing abstract thought; before that religion was impossible. But the community is far older; man is a communal animal, and before man the system of community was fully developed by most varieties of animals, who find in it the best protection against their foes. When we look at these animal communities we see intolerance has the fullest sway, as the essential feature in common action. Every communal animal, from ants up to elephants, has a violent intolerance against those that do not belong to its community. And this is the very safeguard of the system, as without it outsiders would claim the benefits of protection and help without any obligation to render the same in return.

We then reach the position that Intolerance is as old as communal action in the animal world, giving the necessary cohesion to that action; and we notice that all animals have tests for intolerance, they examine others by smell, by appearance, by memory, to decide whether they are of the same stock or no. A test is needful for the action of this great safeguard. Now, when men became capable of religion, of abstract ideas, and of inherited beliefs, such proved at once to be far the most decisive test of the community. If a man thought as you did about what he could not learn by his senses, he must have acquired his ideas in your own tribe, and belong to you. Hence Religion became the conclusive test of community, and animal Intolerance adopted the human acquirement of Religion as its most effective way to distinguish friends from enemies.

4. Thus Religion has nothing essentially intolerant in it; but the detestation of those who hold different opinions is merely the instinct of the herd transferred to those matters of opinion which give it the most effective definition.

In this point of view we see at once how it can be that intolerance is so strong and masterful an instinct. It has been necessary to the welfare of the community—and hence also of the individual—during the greater part of the history of animal life on the earth. And the desperate vigour of wars of religion is because they are the descendants of those struggles which each animal has made to preserve its own species. The prominence and sacredness of initiation to people of all grades of religion is thus explained: on reaching independence it is needful for each individual to be put in possession of all the inherited beliefs which serve to prove his right to the protection of his community, and to test the claims of others upon his own assistance. This subject has necessarily only been sketched in the shortest way here as a preliminary to our next consideration.

5. What the results are of a fusion of races upon their beliefs have to be noticed before we can deal with the construction of the Egyptian religion. In considering this the modern fusions of race are unfortunately not examples to the point; nearly all modern fusions that we can examine being between monotheism and polytheism, and in such the exclusive claims of monotheism leave but scanty ground for the previous polytheism in any form.

But turning to the ancient world, there are some good examples for study. The Greek settlers in Egypt, we find, largely adopted Egyptian gods; for instance, Aristoneikos appears on his stele as a mummy introduced by Anubis to the presence of Osiris and Isis; and the mummy-case of Artemidoros is covered with figures of Anubis, Osiris, Isis, Nebhat, &c. As a whole, the Greek settlers in their day appear to have readily adopted both Egyptian customs and Egyptian gods. On the other hand, Greek gods were freely worshipped in Egypt wherever Greek population was in force. There seems to have been no obstacle to the free acceptance of each other's mythology, after the initial question of fusion of the races was settled. The Greeks adopted as their great local god for the new city of Alexandria the deified Hapi, which had been worshipped as a bull at Memphis; and they recognized him as a god that died and was renewed by calling him the Osirian, Osir-hapi, or Serapis. The human form that was given him made him practically a Greek Zeus, and so ensured his acceptance by the Greek world.

Looking at earlier times in Egypt, we see the same process. After the fusion of the Egyptian and Syrian races in the XVIIIth Dynasty, Syrian gods, Baal, Ashteroth,

Anaitis, and others, were freely worshipped in Egypt, probably by the mixed descendants of the two races.

Again, in the West we can trace similar results. In Gaul and Britain we find side by side altars to Keltic and to Latin deities; neither of them excluded the other, and the mixed descendants of legionaries and natives worshipped the gods of either side.

When we turn to the fusions in which monotheism takes one part, we find considerable signs of the same results, in spite of its exclusiveness. In ancient Judaism so long as any fusion of race was allowed the worship of the gods of both sides was freely followed; and we find Manasseh building altars to all the host of heaven in the temple of Yahveh at Jerusalem. (2 Kings xxi. 5.) It is only by the most rigid racial separation (Ezra x. 11, &c.) that a fusion of religion was prevented in later times. The same thing is obvious in the history of Christianity; the polytheism of the ancestors of the mixed races has never been eradicated; the Keltic fairies were quite as real to the men of past generations as any of the saints, and many a man would sooner brave the terrors of the church than insult the local spirits of the moor or river. What we superciliously call superstitions are the fossilized religion of our ancestors; and we see every day now around us men who are far more annoyed by thirteen at dinner than by breaking any precept of the Sermon on the Mount, and who believe in charms, luck, and other barbaric notions quite as strongly as in any element of their professed religion. The same is seen when we look at races which have recently adopted Christianity; on all sides, from Africa, from Siberia, from New Zealand, we hear that the old beliefs are hardly impaired, and on any great trouble or danger the venerated customs and incantations and offerings have their full sway. In Hayti, where the negro has his own way, there appears to be a complete equality of the old and new beliefs.

6. From this review of examples of mixture we may conclude that the usual law is that one religion does not supplant another, but is only superadded to it, the old and the new being each impaired by only receiving a partial support. Also that in a fusion of race there is a complete mixture of religion; and in a change of civilization an adoption of much of the new

beliefs. And that the question of which shall be predominant depends on the general predominance of the race or civilization at any point in question. But Intolerance assures us that a mixture of race and a mixture of religion will always accompany each other, excepting, perhaps, in a few cases of an overwhelming influence of a great civilization.

Closely connected with this is the difference between a popular and a priestly religion. In every country we see two editions of what professes to be the same faith; one used in the household or family life, the other in public worship under the direction of the state. This divergence is generally due to the state religion belonging to a later importation of a ruling race, while the domestic religion retains more of the aboriginal type. We may see this among ourselves where many ideas of a future state commonly accepted belong evidently to Keltic or Saxon faiths, and have no root whatever in the doctrines of the Church. And we note the result of the same action in the Teutonic ideas of equality which are inherent in the Nonconformist rebellion against that priestly character of the Church, which is of Latin origin and of Norman enforcement.

So we may reasonably expect to find more of the native parts of a religion showing in the popular and domestic worship; while the later elements will be stronger in the official worship. Thus the divergence between these two may serve as a test of the relative ages of different articles of belief.

On another point we have little or no data to positively guide us; but it seems not unlikely that older beliefs when partially overgrown with newer will gradually force their way into prominence again, while the newer will fade in importance. This may be surmised when we note that a conquered race always subdues its conquerors to its own type after a few centuries of fusion. The Lombard-Italians, the Norman-French, the Anglo-Irish, illustrate this. And what is true of the races is probably true of the religions. Hence when a particular belief which belongs to the people steadily wins its way against more ostentatious and dominant worship, there is a fair presumption that it belongs to the other stratum, which has been temporarily overlaid.

We have now endeavoured to reach some ideas of the phenomena of mixture in religion; and to gain some guide by which we may interpret what we notice in considering the Egyptian religion in its historical aspect.

7. When we look to the evidences of the various races which together formed the population of Egypt at the earliest historical age, we are able to glean some valuable hints, mainly from the portraiture. Three distinct types are met with on the sculptures of the IVth Dynasty. The ruling race is akin to the type of the people of Punt, the "divine land"; and it seems most probable that the dynastic Egyptians entered the Nile valley at Koptos from the Red Sea. Another type found in high position is akin to the early Mesopotamian heads from Tell Lo; and it is generally recognized that there are so many traces of influence from that region that an immigration thence is a probable factor. Thirdly, there is a coarse type of a mulatto appearance; and as it is certain anatomically that there is much negro blood in the oldest Egyptians, we have one element of the mulatto in evidence. The light element is doubtless Libyan, be-

cause throughout historic times invasions from the West have occurred every few centuries, and they are not likely to have originated at the rise of Egyptian power: also the negroes are most likely to have mixed with the fair races which bounded their region in the North. This has been stated at length in the History (i. 12-15), and need not, therefore, be more fully entered on here.

We have thus to expect a first stratum of negro and Libyan, then a Mesopotamian influence, and lastly a Punite power, in the religions as also in the races.

LECTURE II.

THE POPULAR RELIGION OF EGYPT

8. From the scarcity of objects of domestic worship belonging to early times, it is difficult to trace the popular religion on the material side, as we can study the official religion upon the monuments. It is nevertheless the most important source that we can have for understanding the early beliefs, as it probably represents the religion of an earlier type than that officially adopted. Happily we have a tolerable outline of it embodied in the priceless series of tales, which reveal to us so much of Egyptian life.

The first thing that strikes us in the tales is that the gods are by no means omniscient nor omnipotent. There appear to be three independent powers—the gods, fate, and man; and each of these can act irrespective of the others.

The powers of man are expressed in magic; and in this we see what is probably the very earliest form of belief. The lack of realizing what the limits of natural action are, the readiness to credit exceptional persons with powers which we do not possess, is one of the most frequent errors of the uninstructed mind, and one which we may see around us at present. In all the earliest tales the magician is the mainspring of the action. He can make magical animals by modelling them, and make them live and act, or return to their original material at his will. He can resuscitate decapitated animals. He can divide the river, and descend to its bed. There is nothing that is impossible to him in dealing either with inert or with living matter. So far there is nothing spiritual in question, but simply the limit of man's control over matter and life, which appears to be quite undefined, and to be credited with any amount of extension. Such was the belief in the Old Kingdom to which the writing of these tales belongs.

When we look at later tales we do not find magic predominant until the Ptolemaic age. At that time the physical magic of the early times reappears in full force. A magic cabin with men and tackle is made to work under water; and a magical recitation can make the dead to speak, although it cannot restore them to life. Magic is also connected at this time with powers over that which is out of reach, so that all that is beyond our ken should be perceived by eye and ear; the birds of the air, and the fish of the deep are to be understood, and the dead shall hear and see all that the living perceive and do, by means of these magic spells. This bears the general character of the later magic of the Gnostics.

9. Regarding the soul, we do not glean any belief from the earlier tales. The king's soul is referred to as a hawk, in the XIIth Dynasty, and again in the XIXth; thus explaining the hawk which is figured over the king's *ka* name, as being his soul or *ba*. The combination of the human-headed bird for the *ba* of ordinary men is doubtless later than the belief in the royal *ba* being a hawk; later because it would be the more noble to have a human head than a bird's head, and the hawk must have been firmly attached to the theory of the royal soul before the half-human form was devised for all men; also later because the supposition of the soul flitting as a bird would precede the invention of a monstrous form

to represent it. How early the *ba*-bird was invented is not known. The oldest representations of it are not before the New Kingdom; and as in that age we find another belief about the soul, it seems as if the *ba*-bird was not universally accepted at that time.

This other belief is that the soul could be taken out of the body at will, and placed in any other position; in this case of Bata it was hidden on the top of a tree. While the soul was thus deposited, the life of the man was independent of what might occur to his body; but he fell down dead if the seat of his soul was destroyed. This belief is spread from the Celts to the Chinese, and is, therefore, a standard piece of psychology. But as we do not meet with it elsewhere in Egypt, and it is antagonistic to the *ba* theory, it is more likely not to belong to Egypt, but to have been imported from Asia Minor along with the rest of the Atys myth in which it appears.

The *ka* is not alluded to in the tales until Ptolemaic times, although we know from monuments that the belief in it belongs to the earliest religion. We gain, however, an enlarged idea of it from its action in the tale of Setna. There a *ka* has the affections of its former life, and it will wander hundreds of miles from its own tomb to dwell in the tomb of its mate. Yet it is uneasy at being so separated from its own tomb, as the union of the two burials is desired by it. The *ka* is equally visible, and viable whether in its own place or any other. It can talk and describe the past; it can argue, it can play games with mortals, it can inflict supernatural penalties. But its powers cease where physical force is concerned; Setna, after stories, arguments, and gaming have been tried on him in vain, takes by force the roll which he covets, simply reaching out his hand for the book and taking it. Thus, while the senses, the memory, the speech, discernment, and motion are all credited to the *ka*, and we begin to wonder in what it differs from the living person, the touch of simple force undoes its powers at once. It has then all the full properties of mind, but not the abilities to act with force upon matter. Though this is a very late account of the *ka*, yet it accords well with the partial light on its nature that we have on the older monuments. The whole motive of tomb decoration was to provide a home for the *ka*, furnished with all good things. The models and images of the food and furniture, servants and estates, are the equivalent of the realities to the mind; and as the *ka* cannot exercise force upon matter, the provision of actual matter is not required. No doubt this is a logical refinement on the primitive offering of the cake of bread and jar of water, such as we find in the earliest tombs, and such as is still presented after six thousand years in the tombs of the fellahin now. There the actual material without any theorizing is placed by the body for its sustenance, and its sandals and staff for its long journey lie by it. And as the offering is still now made, so probably it had been made for thousands of years before the earliest burials that we know. The dogma of the *ka* using these offerings without any material diminution of them, and its satisfaction with the images of the offerings, is evidently a later conception; while yet we see the earlier idea in its most primitive simplicity lasting until the present day.

10. So far we have dealt with man and his parts; we now turn to the supernatural forces around him. Closely linked with the

belief in the *ka* and *ba* was the worship of the tree spirit. In many representations we have the tree goddess in various forms—human, cow-headed, or shown as a mere arm emerging from the branches of the sycomore, and pouring out blessings on the kneeling *ka* and the bowing *ba* bird. The sustenance of the parts of the dead was attributed to the beneficent tree spirit, and hence the widespread veneration of the sycomore in every home, and more particularly about Memphis with its vast cemetery of Sakkara, where the great sycomore of the south was a noted feature. It is alluded to in the XIIth Dynasty as a well-known point in the country. This group of ideas of the *ka*, *ba*, and sycomore spirit, was associated with the domestic worship, and perhaps formed the main part of it. In the Ramesseum dwellings a niche in the wall has this group painted in it; another such niche has a flight of steps leading up to it as a sacred place, and similar niches are found in the private houses of Tell el Amarna. The focus of domestic worship then appears to have been a niche or false door in the wall of the principal hall, usually in the west wall like the false doors of tombs; this was dignified with steps in some cases, and painted with the objects of adoration, the ancestral double and spirit, *ka* and *ba*, and the tree-genius who preserved them.

The tree is named as the residence of a human spirit in the XIXth Dynasty, when Bata places his soul on a tree to preserve it, and drops dead himself when the tree is cut down. Again, he is transformed into two trees, and speaks from a tree to his wicked wife. Hence it seems that a tree with its thick hiding foliage and deep shade was thought to be particularly a suitable abode for both human and divine spirits; and "the sycomore of the south" is called the living body of Hathor.

Offerings were made to trees, evidently to propitiate the spirit which dwelt in them; the peasant is figured bowing to the sycomore in his field, and surrounding it with jars of drink offerings; and when Bata is transformed into two Persea trees, "there were offerings made to them."

What divinities were associated with trees is a very variable point. The Sycomore has always a goddess, generically described as Hathor, or specifically as Nut, Selk, or Neit.

This variation shows that the tree does not belong to any of these deities in particular, but is only the residence of a beneficent tree-goddess, who was identified with any goddess that was prominent. In fact it belongs to a different religion to that of these human goddesses, and was combined with them afterwards. In one case a god is named, when a tall palm is identified with Tahuti.

11. The part that animals hold in the religion is important, yet we find very little trace of it in the tales. In the earliest time a crocodile is always the minister of vengeance, but is not regarded as divine. In the XIIth Dynasty the serpents of the enchanted island talk, and in the XIXth Dynasty the kine of Bata talk. The first case is however a part of distant marvels; and the second probably means that Bata was so observant and sympathetic with his cattle, that their actions were like speech to him. It does not then seem that talking animals, which are so familiar in other beliefs, had any real place in Egyptian ideas. The worship of the sacred bull appears in the tale of Bata; and there a great feast is made to the animal god just

before he is killed. That killing the god was part of the religion we can well believe when we see it in other countries ; and even in Egypt a ram was killed yearly at Thebes, and the statue of Amen covered with its skin. The actual remains of the bulls found in the Serapeum by Mariette show that in the XIXth Dynasty they were consumed by the worshippers, as is shown by Bata's wife eating the bull's liver. That the slaughter of venerated animals was not discordant to Egyptian ideas, we also see by the death of the cow which had been specially selected and brought up as a mate to the Apis bull, but which was killed immediately after consorting with him. The Egyptian regarded a continuity of life as so assured through the *ka* and the *ba*, that it did not make much break in the life for it to be transferred from one state to the other.

Other popular worships of animals are seen in the treatment of the sacred serpent or good genius of buildings and places ; and the serpent goddess of agriculture Renent, who was adored with offerings. This is probably a very primitive worship, as also that of the cynocephali baboons, with their solemn faces, which gave them the credit of the embodiment of wisdom, and their activity at sunrise, when they were supposed to adore the sun-god.

12. Of the purely spiritual conceptions is that of the fates, who predict an enigmatical future for the man at his birth. In the early time the goddess Meskhent—a birth-deity—predicts the future of the infant; but in the New Kingdom we see that a group of goddesses, generically termed Hathors, are present and give an oracular utterance which may have several interpretations. They appear to see a part of the future, to be able to assign the limits of its uncertainties, but not to control or regulate it in the least. Much of the choice of the future lies with man himself; his own foresight and ingenuity is to help him; yet he cannot step beyond certain limits where his fate meets him, and bounds his freedom of action. This is a very practical version of the limited freedom of action which men possess; reconciling the apparent ability of man to determine his condition, with the ruthless chapter of accidents which binds him. He has a certain course and end broadly assigned to him, within the limits of which he can

modify his life and rule his state. When he has overcome one of the possibilities of evil which beset him, he is thenceforth free of that risk for the future, "Thy god has given one of thy dooms into thy hand." This conception would seem to have arisen from a man overcoming some particular temptation which might be a doom to him, and so being delivered from its overwhelming him in future.

13. We lastly turn to what views the people had of their gods. In the Old Kingdom tales we find Ra supreme; but that is to be expected, as the Vth Dynasty, which is in question, is described as being descended from Ra, and called its kings "Sons of Ra." Ra there orders the other deities, Isis and Nebhat, the osiride goddesses, Meskhent, the name goddess, Hekt, the goddess of birth, and Khnumu, the creative god, who gives strength to the limbs of the new-born. All of these deities are purely human in form, and they appear as a party of travelling dancing girls with a porter. It is evident, then, that the osiride group were the prominent human divinities—as distinguished from the cosmic Ra—at that time; and that the domestic deities of

creation and birth were familiar to the Egyptian. But no marvels are attributed to them beyond the control of the weather, and the making of models of royal crowns which gave out a sound of festivity afterwards when hidden.

In a later time we find in the New Kingdom Ra is appealed to as a deliverer, who can interpose obstacles to an unjust attack. And swearing by Ra-Harakhti was the regular form of a strong asseveration of the truth, as it occurs in two tales.

Beside Ra, we find in the XIXth Dynasty an Ennead, or group of nine gods, who are popularly supposed to walk together on the earth to view all that passes. Ra-Harakhti is at the head of this group, and Khnumu is of the company; but the remainder are unspecified, and as the well-known enneads do not contain Khnumu we cannot be certain who was implied in this, or, indeed, if any gods were referred to in particular. Probably it only implies the principal gods in general. But it is remarkable that they do not rule immovable in heaven, but walk together on the earth "to look upon the whole land." Khnumu, the potter who forms mankind on his wheel, here frames a non-human woman, who is devoid of all natural feeling or passions, and has but a craving for power.

On reaching the Ptolemaic times we get further light on the popular conceptions of the gods. When Na-nefer-ka-ptah by magic obtains the hidden book of Thoth, it takes apparently a day or two for Thoth to discover the loss. He is therefore dependent upon sources of information, and is not omniscient. Next he goes to Ra to complain; Ra therefore is not omniscient. And Ra gives Thoth permission to punish Na-nefer-ka-ptah; Thoth therefore cannot avenge himself without permission. Next, neither of the gods can act directly by his will upon man or matter, as Ra "sent a power from heaven with the command" to injure Na-nefer-ka-ptah. This introduces another conception, that of angels or messengers, which became so important in gnosticism and Christianity. The power accordingly acts at once, and evil ensues, the child is drowned. The drowned child can be forced into speech by reading magic spells over him; and in this state he can reveal what the gods had done. This suggests the idea that the news of the spiritual world goes round from mouth to mouth as in this world; and when a spirit once went there the acts of the gods became known to it.

Thus we see that the belief in the gods was entirely different from modern ideas. They were neither self-informed nor self-acting; but they depended on information received, and they acted through messengers. This may be a later form of belief, as in earlier times we see Bata calling on Ra, and Ra directly listening to him and attending to his needs.

Passing now from the tales we may glean somewhat about the popular beliefs from the lesser remains, such as private tablets and little figures of gods, which are frequently found, and yet which are some of them of different type to anything pourtrayed in the temples. The serpent-worship of the goddess Renent Nebtka, the divinity of cultivation, is shown at a harvest festival. A great heap of the grain is piled up before her; the long-handled shovels and forks and the winnowing scrapers are stuck upright into the heap as being done with; two men are still piling on the grain from measures which they carry; while beyond, the winnowers are finishing the winnowing over another heap of grain. This is a scene of the beginning of the XIXth Dynasty, and shows a popular festival of that time.

14. The ivory wands covered with incised figures belonging to the Middle Kingdom show a large number of deities and genii, which have more connection with the Book of the Dead than with any state worship. Among these the great cat, who is in the Persea tree of Heliopolis, the Mehurt cow, and the eye of Horus, all belong to the XVIIth chapter, which is considered one of the earliest. Beside these there are shown Taurt devouring a captive; Bes, both in male and female form, holding serpents; Taurt and Sekhet devouring serpents; and Set. The tortoise, frog, and scarab appear; and several monsters, as a serpent-headed leopard; hawk-headed leopard winged, with a human head between the wings; sphinx; and winged uraeus. These figures are akin to those monsters represented at Beni Hasan. This group of supernatural figures gives an outline of the commonly received ideas, apparently connected with the coming forth from Duat, or the under-world, like the XVIIth chapter,

which has evidently a connection with these carvings.

Coming to later times one of the most usual objects of popular worship is a small stele or tablet with Horus on the crocodiles. In the earliest form, about the XVIIIth-XIXth Dynasty (basalt tablet, F.P. coll.), Horus is a hunter armed with bow and quiver; we see then that the animals must be those which he has slain. As Maspero has pointed out, all the animals figured were supposed to fascinate man, the lion, oryx, scorpion, serpent, and crocodile; and Horus conquered them to protect man. Next, in the XXIInd Dynasty, we have a similar idea of Ptah-Sokar, the deformed pigmy figure, who stands on crocodiles, and grasps serpents in his hands. These serpents sometimes are figured as being half in his mouth, with only the tails out. This is another view of the protection against serpents by eating them, which is the common practice of South African people at present, and probably of all serpent charmers. Experiments very completely performed with serpent poisons, and just published, show that doses of poison and also of serpent's blood taken internally confer on the eater immunity from the effects of injected poison, such as that infused by bites. The Ptah-Sokar eating serpents is, therefore, overcoming them in another way. In the later Ptolemaic times, tablets of Horus on the crocodiles are very common, crowded on the back and sides with inscriptions which have neither accuracy nor meaning. Such tablets abound just when the use of other amulets came into common fashion, and they lead on to the great belief in amulets in gnostic times. We see then here an important element of popular religion in these tablets, which were to serve for the protection of the owner from noxious animals.

15. The main worship of the people in the later times of the Greek and Roman occupations seems to have been concentrated upon Isis and Horus. The innumerable cheap terra-cotta figures of Horus in all forms, are the commonest objects of the Roman period. With a hole in the back to hang on a peg in the wall, they were placed in the huts of the poorest of the people; their cost must have been so minute that none would be so poor as not to own one. No other god seems to have had such popularization, and even Isis and Serapis come far behind Horus in their general acceptance. Broadly speaking, the

Egyptians were a Horus-worshipping people in Roman times, honouring Isis also as his mother; and the influence that this had on the development of Christianity was profound. We may even say that but for the presence of Egypt we should never have seen a Madonna. Isis had obtained a great hold on the Romans under the earlier Emperors, her worship was fashionable and wide-spread; and when she found a place in the other great movement, that of the Galileans, when fashion and moral conviction could shake hands, then her triumph was assured, and, as the Mother Goddess, she has ruled the devotion of Italy ever since. How much Horus has entered into the popular development of Christianity—how the figure of the Divine Teacher, set in a sad, stern frame of Semitic and Syrian influence, has become changed into the rampant baby of Correggio—is seen readily when we note the general popular worship of the child Horus, and see that passing over into the rising influence of Christianity. In one small particular there is much significance. The well-known Christian monogram (*khi-rho*) may be seen in course of gradual formation in Egypt—or possibly in course of alteration;

but the *rho* is usually figured as an upright staff with the lock of Horus at the top, and not the letter *rho*. Essentially it is the sign of Horus, and only became Christian by adoption.

We have now briefly gone over the various elements of popular religion in Egypt, as distinct from that of the temples; religion which was far less influenced by political and other changes, and was really the vital belief of the greater part of the inhabitants. It is simpler than the official and priestly worship, and has a much greater vitality. Buried in the hearts of millions, changes could not uproot it, and with nominal modifications, and with new ideals implanted in it, the old framework has largely kept its hold down to the present time, excepting where the violent monotheism of Islam has crushed it. The conquests of Islam were not so much over Christianity as over the elder paganism, which had retained its hold and its position; and it was that alone which gave force and point to the invectives of Muhammed against the far older Tritheism, Mariolatry, and Saint-worship which went by the name of Christianity in his times.

LECTURE III.

THE DISCORDANCES OF EGYPTIAN RELIGION

16. The discordances and contradictions in any religion are one of the most important evidences of its history. The ruling idea of most religious beliefs is the need of accounting for something, and of explaining the mysteries of life. Hence beliefs which explain the unseen in a totally different way and with different ideals will not be needlessly produced at a single source. Some new influence must be at work to cause diversity; and when two views live on side by side with partial fusion, it is—like instances of two mythologies—an evidence of a mixture of peoples who had held varying opinions.

This discrepancy in belief is most characteristic of Egypt, and we need to disentangle the elements before we can venture to classify them.

Concerning the future state of man there were at least three wholly contradictory theories; the Earthly, the Elysian, and the Solar theories: and it is probable that the mummy theory is a fourth.

The Earthly theory was that of the *ka*, or double, which, as we have seen, had the feelings and the activities of life, only limited by the inability to act on matter. This *ka* required a supply of food, in the form of continually renewed offerings, for which a place of offering was provided in front of the doorway which led to the tomb-pit. Up that pit from the sepulchre passed the *ka*, and also the *ba* or soul, and coming out through the imitation door that was provided it fed on the offerings which were laid on the altar in front of the door. Soon a recess was made for the altar by added coatings to the mastaba that developed into a chamber, and then that chamber was elaborated into a dwelling for the *ka*, its walls were covered with figures of offerings and of servants, and large granaries and store-rooms were provided in it. Being incapable of acting on matter, the image of an offering was as good as the object itself to the *ka*; and so the continually renewed offerings of the earliest times became changed for the permanent pictures of the offerings. This view of the *ka* and the *ba* was associated with the tree-spirit worship, and these together formed a domestic worship, which was associated with niches or figures of doorways in dwellings where the ancestors were adored. All of this theory implies a continued after-life upon the earth, dependent on earthly support.

17. The Elysian theory was entirely independent of any connection with the earth. The dead became the subjects of the great god of the dead, Osiris; they lived in Aalu, a mythic land beyond the ken of man, at first supposed to be on earth or later on in heaven. There they navigated on the canals, they tilled the soil, they planted, they watered, they reaped. And admission to this duplicate of earthly life was obtained by a test of weighing the heart to see if it were true and right, and denying the commission of all earthly sins before the judgment-seat of Osiris. Here we have a totally different theory, and one which left no time or opportunity for the *ka* to wander on this earth, and no need for it to be provided with earthly sustenance.

The Solar theory was equally independent

of both of the others. The deceased flew up to the sun, and joined the solar bark : he passed through all the perils of the night under the protection of Ra, and emerged into new day at sunrise. For ever he dwelt with Ra, and shared his dangers by night and his success by day.

18. Now, none of these theories, it will be observed, requires the mummy. The Elysian and Solar theories ignore the body on earth ; and the figure of the deceased in the Osirian judgment is always as a living person, and not a mummy. It is only in the age of greatest confusion and mixture, under the Ptolemies and Emperors, that the mummy is supported by Anubis into the presence of Osiris. The *ka* and *ba* theory might involve the preservation of the mummy ; and in the comparatively late age of the New Kingdom the *ba* flies down the tomb-pit to the mummy, and the *ba* lingers longingly on the breast of the mummy pleading to return to its place. But the earlier evidence may make us doubt whether mummification were an original part of the *ka* and *ba* theory. Why, for example, should the *ka* require sustenance if the mummified body remains unaltered and imperishable? And at the beginning

of the IVth Dynasty mummification was at a point of elaborate resemblance to the living body, by modelling in resin, a system which rapidly deteriorated a few generations later; such a history indicates that it was a somewhat recent introduction, whereas the *ka* and *ba* theory is probably of the earliest race and age, before the Elysian or Solar theories. It seems, then, probable that the mummifying may belong to another theory—that of revivification, with which it is always associated by writers; whereas there is neither place nor purpose in any bodily revivification in the *ka* theory or the Elysian or Solar theories. There are then certainly three, and perhaps four, views about the soul which have no original unity, but rather show a complete discordance, apparently due to different origins and races.

19. Now, as there are diversities in the beliefs about the soul, so there are like diversities in the beliefs about the divinities. It is familiar how confused the mythology is owing to parallel gods—alike, yet distinct; and fused gods—unalike, yet combined; how a god would be in power at one time and rejected at another. All this change is vaguely put down to local influences, which

is only the first step in tracing the causation. Differences between neighbouring places in their fundamental beliefs are not mere senseless vagaries; they imply a difference between the people—that is, a difference in race. According to most Egyptologists the variety of gods was determined by the different beliefs of every petty capital of every province of Egypt. Yet these authorities avoid the conclusion that these gods belong to different ancestries. Let us just see what this position requires of us. If the gods arise without difference of ancestry in their worshippers—and it is admitted that all the principal gods are far prehistoric—then we have the view that there existed in Egypt a unified mass of population, which had mingled without having any previous mythologies; and subsequently in Egypt they evolved different gods at many different centres. This is what is generally tacitly assumed, even by Maspero, who sees the perspective of the history of mythology far more than any other authority. But such a view requires us to believe that for long ages, while these gods were being evolved and brought into contact in Egypt, not a single serious immigration of foreign races had taken place. In short, that though the known history of Egypt shows a great influx of neighbouring people every few centuries, we are asked to suppose that such mixtures were quite insignificant in all the far longer prehistoric ages, while the gods were in course of evolution. Such a view, thus reduced to historic parallelism, is an insult to our sense of probability.

20. That great mixtures of race had taken place in the prehistoric ages, probably oftener than once in a thousand years, is practically certain, when we view the known history. And as such mixtures always produce local diversity, we should expect to see differences and incongruities between the beliefs of all the principal, and even the minor, centres of population. In one town the A tribe would be strongest; in the next the B tribe still remained in power; on the opposite side the C tribe had later thrust themselves in. Such is the view which is forced upon us by the historic probabilities of the country. Hence, local differences are only another name for tribal differences and diversities of origin.

It may be said that we do not see such new gods being introduced by the migrations during historic times, and hence we should not expect these changes to result from the prehistoric migrations. This is a very partial view. In the first place new gods were needless, because almost every race that could burst into Egypt had already come in and planted their gods, hence reconquests by the same race a second time merely brought forward their already-present god. To take an acknowledged instance, the Libyan conquest by the XXIInd and XXVIth Dynasties forced Neith, the Libyan goddess, into prominence, after she had almost disappeared in Egypt. When a really fresh race came in their gods then appear also as new gods in Egypt, such as the Syrian gods and the Greek gods. Then, moreover, when once the religion had become fixed by written formulæ and types of worship on monuments, the beliefs already figured on the spot held their ground against the unwritten faith of the moving immigrants.

While, therefore, fully recognizing that the diversities of belief were local, and that the prominence of a deity was largely due to the political importance of his centre of worship, yet we must logically see behind these local differences the racial and tribal differences by which they were caused; and behind the political power of a place we must perceive the political power of the race who dwelt there, and whose beliefs were spread around by their political predominance. Amen-worship spread from Thebes, or Neit-worship from Sais, not merely because those places were the seat of power, but because the people of those places who worshipped Amen and Neit extended their power and dwelt as governors and officials in the rest of the country. It is race and not place that is the real cause of change.

21. One of the best known incongruities is the position of Set. In the earliest times Set and Horus appear as co-equal or twin-gods (M.E.E., 329) closely associated. In the VIIIth Chapter of the Book of the Dead the deceased, who is usually identified with Osiris, states that he is identical with Set: while, evidently after the antagonistic view of Set and Horus had come in, a sentence was added deprecating the wrath of Horus. Now the possibility of such a view of Set is explained by the earliest history of Horus. Maspero states that Isis was originally the Virgin-mother, dwelling alone as a separate sole goddess at Buto, from whom Horus was self-produced

(M.H.A., 131). The union of Osiris to Isis, and his adoption of Horus, was a later modification. Hence there was no incongruity in the earliest view of Horus and Set being honoured side by side. But when Horus became the step-son of Osiris, later the full son of Osiris himself, he was bound to be antagonistic to Set. That Set belongs to the Libyans or Westerns is probable, because he is considered to have red hair and a white skin; in fact, the Tahennu, or clear-race complexion. And it is probable that the Osiris-Isis group is also of Libyan origin, as we shall see later on.

Hence we may picture to ourselves the gods Isis, Osiris, and Set, as the three divinities of different tribes of Libyans. So long as the Isis worshippers and Set worshippers were in fraternity and tribal union, Horus and Set were coequal gods. But when the Osiris worshippers, with whom the Setites were at feud, united with the Isiac tribe, and Osiris was married to Isis, it became the duty of Horus to fight Set. Accordingly we see the war of Horus and Set throughout Egypt, and garrisons of the followers of Horus were established by the side of the principal centres of Set worship to keep down the Setite tribe. (See Masp., Études ii. 324.) This tribal view of the religious discordances and changes seems to be the only rational cause that can be assigned. That tribal wars existed no one would venture to dispute, and that religious changes would ensue from political changes we see exemplified all through the history of Egypt. The cause existed for such divergences, and it was capable of producing these divergences: while no other reasonable cause can be assigned, and the gods are expressly represented as fighting and vanquishing each other's followers. We need hardly say that the Syrian god Sutekh, which comes in about the XIXth Dynasty, has no connection with the primitive Egyptian god Set.

22. Another puzzling and discordant element in the mythology is the goddess Hathor. She is the most ubiquitous deity of all. Yet she is seldom worshipped alone and unmodified, and she is usually identified with some other goddess or with a female form of some god. Sekhet, Neit, Iusaas, Best, Uazit, Mut, Hekt, and Aset are all identified with her at different places, and she appears as female forms of Sopd, Behudt, Anpu, and Tanen. She has no permanent

characteristics, no special attributes. The uncouth human face with cow's ears and modified cow's horns is the only typical form of the goddess, and the cow and the sistrum are her only emblems; but these distinctions are not constant. Worshipped in every nome of Upper and Lower Egypt, she was yet one of the most evasive deities, and most easily modified and combined.

Let us reflect on what this indicates. That the worship was thus general, equally diffused over the country, points to the country having been under a uniform condition of subjection to her worshippers. While the fact that at no centre is she solely worshipped, and at very few places even prominently, points to other deities having been already in possession of the country when her devotees spread her adoration. Where then are we to look for her native land? It has been shown that Hathor was lady of Punt, and was thence introduced into Egypt. And we may see further confirmation of this. The only places outside of Egypt with which she is connected are Punt, Mafekt (Sinai)—where the Punites are very likely to have settled on the Red Sea — and Kapna. This last is usually rendered as equal to the Gubla or Byblos, but another Kapna was in the land of Punt, and in the only place where Hathor is lady of Kapna she is also lady of Wawat on the Upper Nile. (Rec. II. 120.) Hence it is more likely that the Kapna of Hathor is a district of Punt. Further, of Isis, who is identified at Dendera with Hathor, it is said, "Isis was born in the Iseum of Dendera of Apt, the great one of the temple of Apt, under the form of a woman black and red." (M. Dend. text 30.) This points to a southern origin. The Punites are coloured dark red, and the neighbouring peoples black, while the Asiatics are yellow, and the Libyans fair. When we come to look to the nature of the goddess we see further connection. That Min was a Punite god is most likely, as his position at Koptos on the Red Sea road indicates, as well as his three colossal statues there, apparently carved by a Red Sea people in prehistoric time. And Min was the great father-god. Hathor is the co-relative mother-god, she in whom dwells the son Hor. Her character as the universal mother is well recognized, and is plainly on a par with the idea of Min as the great father. Thus the two gods whom we are led to connect with the Punite race by their position, are similar in nature and point to a worship of reproduction apparently belonging to that people. Another connection is seen in the position of Hathor in the country. The only supreme centre for her was at Dendera, which is opposite to Koptos, the seat of Min, and on the line of any invaders from the Red Sea into the Nile valley.

That Hathor was brought in by a people after the establishment of the other deities we have already observed. And this exactly agrees to her belonging to the Punite race which founded the dynastic history. Their great female divinity they identified with every other goddess that they met throughout Egypt, and established her worship also as a local Hathor in every nome, calling her the "princess of the gods." The whole phenomena of the diffusion of her worship are thus accounted for by the historical connection in which her origin leads us to place her. Therefore, by her being stated to come from Punt, by the foreign places to which she is connected, by her colour, by her being complementary to Min the other Punite god, by the place of her main sanctuary, and by the peculiar diffusion of her worship, we are led to one conclusion throughout—that Hathor was the Punite goddess introduced at the beginning of the dynastic history.

23. Another prominent case of discordance is in the worship of the crocodile god Sebek. This was most prevalent in the Fayum, "the lake of the crocodile"; and the marshy, shallow margins of the wide lake as it then was must have been very favourable to such amphibia. Up the Nile other places were also devoted to crocodile worship, such as Silsileh, Ombos, and Nubt, while at neighbouring towns the animal was detested and attacked, as at Dendera, Apollinopolis, and Heracleopolis.

Here such discordant beliefs could not be supposed to spring up side by side amongst a homogeneous people living together; on the contrary, they show a difference of thought and of belief which must have been developed at different places and under different conditions. Sebek was a creative god; being the largest and most intelligent animal of the water, the crocodile was the emblem of the ruler of the primordial ocean. And in later times Osiris was identified with the crocodile, and appears as the reptile with a human head in the

Fayum. As it is impossible for the crocodile worship to have originated outside of Egypt, we may look on it as one of the oldest worships in the country, as the people who adopted such a belief cannot have had any other very fixed or developed worship already adopted. That it originated in the Fayum is possible from its permanence there, from that being a great haunt of crocodiles in early times, and from a western goddess, Neith, being figured as suckling two crocodiles. The seats of Sebek-worship elsewhere in Egypt might, if so, point to migrations of the tribe who occupied the Fayum in the earliest times.

We have now seen enough of these examples of discordant beliefs to credit the view that they are an evidence of the differences of race, and of the various elements of the religion having been introduced by different tribes from various quarters, who had successively forced their way into Egypt.

24. Before going further it will be well to note some of the instances of changes in the religion, and of one belief altering or superseding another, which are already observed and acknowledged by the best

students. The following illustrations are all taken from the studies published by Maspero, who well recognizes that "a religion always has a history, at whatever time after its origin we may view it," and that a study of isolated gods must always precede the treatment of their combined forms.

Of the creative gods there are three—Khnum, Sebek, and Ptah—which do not correspond to the same view of creation, and reigned over different worshippers, at least at first. They were completely strangers, and sometimes enemies, with no more connection than had the princes of the very different districts of Egypt to which they belonged. And even Ptah had a long history, for Tatnen is the oldest form of Ptah; or rather as we should say, a previous god of Memphis, who was absorbed in the later god Ptah, and whose memory was kept up by the compound god Ptah-Tatnen. Ptah was alone at first, and subsequently Sekhet was brought in to the Memphite worship as the wife of Ptah, although her previous position was with Atmu of Heliopolis. Imhotep was at first an epithet of Ptah, before being made into a separate god as the son of Ptah.

Turning to the Heliopolitan gods the changes and growth are frequent. Shu, who was at first space or air, was made into a son of Atmu; then later he became identified with Atmu. In the later growth of the Ra worship some kept to only a human figure of Ra, and a hawk-headed Horakhti; others brought in new names for the new conceptions—Atmu for the past sun, Khepra for the present sun, &c. Then these again became compounded, as Atmu-Harakhti-Khepra.

At Thebes alterations are also seen. The whole Thebaid was originally subject to Mentu; Amen then came forward, and Mentu was reduced to being a son of Amen.

The gods of the dead varied as much as any. Sokar at Memphis and Mertseger at Thebes were the earliest. The kingdom of Sokar in the west was adopted into the Book of Duat; as also was the kingdom of Osiris in the north, and in the stars. And Sokar became identified with Osiris of the Delta, they both being gods of the dead. Then Osiris became also mingled with Khentamenti of Abydos, another god of the dead. And Osiris was also married to Isis, and established the popular Osirian cycle. After that came the combination of the Osiride and Sokar myths in the various ritual books of the future life, where the increasing solarization can be traced as late as the XXth Dynasty. As Maspero says, "The increasingly intimate connection of Osiris and Ra, gradually mixed both myths and dogmas which had been entirely separate at first. The friends and enemies of each became the friends and enemies of the other, and lost their native character in forming combined personages, in whom the most contradictory elements were mixed, often without succeeding in uniting them."

Later than all these changes, and attempted unification of gods, whose nature or whose territories overlapped, came the great sorting movement of forming triads and enneads in highly artificial orders and combinations, which in their turn led up to the idea of the unity of all the gods, that is so prominent in the later pantheistic views. These latest ideas put forward in the elaborate and lengthy inscriptions of Ptolemaic times are what have led many scholars to lose sight of the several earlier stages which we have here been noticing.

We have now seen how important the discordances and alterations of the Egyptian religion are for throwing some light on the history of its many modifications—a history which passed away before our earliest records, and which can only be recovered by the comparison of different and contradictory views. In these we have embalmed for study the only fragments of the prehistoric age that we can work on; and it is this which gives such study a value far beyond that belonging to the religion alone. We gain a glimpse of the perspective of the growth of mind.

LECTURE IV.

ANALYSIS OF THE EGYPTIAN MYTHOLOGY

25. To anyone attempting to look at first at the mythology of Egypt, the great number of gods and their often complex and ill-defined attributes, render the view most perplexing and repulsive. It appears almost impossible to master the multitude of details, and as if they had little reality and significance when at last understood. We have in the previous sections considered how such a complex subject should be approached, and what the laws are of a mixture of religions; we have then reviewed the popular religion as being the simplest, and showing the point of view of the Egyptian mind; then we have noted the discordances, the contradictions and duplications, and the most obvious changes in mythology, as evidence of its complex origin. Lastly

we now turn to making a brief analysis of the whole mass of supernatural existences which were recognized in Egypt, so as to gain a grasp of the whole material, and to be able to realize its extent and its nature. All of this study may be regarded as prolegomena to the treatment of the mythology in detail; but without such a consideration of principles, and system of classification, we should grope helplessly in the dark, and feel that our view was but partial and imperfect. We may in such a general review as this omit much that is important and overlook many beliefs which were prominent and familiar; but at least we shall see the plan of the whole field and realize its extent and the relation of its parts. It will then remain to explore each myth and trace each deity separately, with the general clue in hand of its position and relation to other beliefs around it.

For this general analysis we may take Lanzone's Mythology as a standard list. No doubt many obscure and derivative spirits may yet be brought to light; but they will only swell the least important section of the mythology. The total number of gods, spirits, and sacred beings or animals in this record is about 438. These may be classified in the following groups :—

Hades, spirits and genii . . 153	
serpents . . . 35	188
Animals, serpents 7	
mammalia, &c. . . 24	31
Monsters	7
Local and minor gods . . .	71
Abstractions	13
Elemental	4
Feminine forms and sons of gods, derived	21
Animal and human compound gods	14
Gods of dead	2
Human gods	11
Cosmic gods	11
Human gods of principles . .	6
varieties of Hathor . .	51
Foreign gods	8
	438

26. The first of these groups is known by the *Book of the Dead*, and other works that deal with the future state, such as the *Book of Knowing Duat*, with its twelve hours of the solar passage; the *Book of Gates* or *Book of Hades*, with its twelve names fenced off by separate portals; the *Book of the opening of the Mouth*, and other

ritual works. These are mostly of a comparatively late date, the *Book of the Dead* being probably the oldest; but in all of them the various stages of the religion are mixed and combined as best they might be. The genii that are met with in these works are therefore of all ages. Some like the great serpent Apap, and the great cat of the Persea tree, may belong to the earliest beliefs; others were added as the need of explanation grew, and many were probably invented for the sake of uniformity, when the consciousness of constructing a systematic guide-book to the unseen was realized by the Egyptian scribes and dogma-makers. Doubtless many of the genii and of the serpents are duplications and subdivisions of the same idea.

27. Of sacred animals we find thirty-one, of which seven are serpents. Four views of this animal worship are now held. Some regard the animals as having been first worshipped for their powers and unexplained actions, simply as fellow-beings with man. Another view is that they were worshipped as exemplifying certain characteristics of power, fertility, cunning, &c. A third view is that they were only sacred to the gods,

and that they were not directly worshipped, except as a corruption in late times. A fourth view is that they were worshipped because of their utility. This last view is certainly not solid, as many of the animals worshipped had no utility to man in any way. The view that they were only emblems of gods, and that the worship of the gods preceded the animal worship is not satisfactory. We see that the tree was sacred before it was connected with a goddess, because many different goddesses are united to tree worship. In the same way different gods are united to the worship of the same animals; the ram is adored for Khnum, for Amen, for Osiris, or for Neit, according to the locality; the bull is connected with Ra, with Osiris, with Set, or with Ptah, and four sacred bulls are specified. Here the presumption certainly is that the trees and animals were sacred already, before they were attached to the worship of one god or other. And, further, we see animals worshipped, and tablets carved to their honour, as animals alone, without any connection with a god, such as the wagtail and the cat; and also adored in preference to the god, as the goose of Amen, the cat of Neit, and the rams of Amen. The view, therefore, that the animals were worshipped independently of the gods, and united to the divine worship subsequently, seems the more reasonable. Whether the abstraction of characteristics preceded animal worship, we cannot say; probably unconsciously it did so, and they were reverenced for their being the greatest exemplification of various qualities. Mysterious intelligence was also attributed to their actions, and the baboon, the ibis, the cat, or the cobra, were each supposed to reason like a man. Remembering the adoration paid both to trees and to serpents at present in Africa, it seems not improbable that we may see the negro element in this plant and animal worship.

Beside animals, various monsters were invented and worshipped; seven such are specified.

28. Then there comes the great mass of local and minor deities, who are only known in a few instances, and who may have held in Egypt much the same place that saints do in Christianity or in Islam. There are several abstractions, which were none of importance; such as the god of Fishers, of Cultivation, of Corn, of Wine, of Earth, of

Fire, of Foreigners, of Writing, of Hearing, of Speech, of Taste, and of Destiny. Most of these are probably of late invention, and have no part in the early systems. There are also elemental gods, and those of Hermopolis, the eight associated with Tahuti. Purely theoretical gods were invented to complete the triads, and twenty-one are feminine forms of a male god, or sons who are otherwise of no importance.

29. We have now passed over more than three-quarters of the spiritual beings: about one hundred remain. Of these half are local forms of Hathor, and eight are foreign, leaving forty-three as the number of important divinities, the great gods as we may call them. These can be divided into four great groups: the partly-animal gods, the essentially human gods (Osirian group), the cosmogonic gods (Ra group), and the gods of human principles. The relative order of the introduction of these groups is as here arranged, so far as we can glean it from their relations to each other. As we have already pointed out, the worship of animals probably preceded that of abstract deities, and hence the half-animal gods are probably older than the others. Then Maspero has shown how

the Osirian doctrine was modified to agree to the solar Ra; and that the heaven created by Horus, and sustained by his four sons, the pillars, is older than the Heliopolitan cosmogony of Ra. The Osirian group of human gods belongs, then, to an older order of things than the cosmogonic gods. Lastly, the fact that Ptah, one of the gods of principles, had to borrow a partner, Sekhet, who was originally the mate of Atmu, and who had a son, Nefertum, points to his being later than the Ra group. And the diffusion of Hathor worship appears to belong to the latest of the prehistoric layers.

Now, without entering on the details at present, it is at least allowable to point out that four successive races in Egypt have been deduced from the examination of the monuments, without looking to any relation to the religion: the Negro, the Libyan, the Mesopotamian, the Punite. And these four races have direct links to the four successive classes of gods which we have just specified. For the present this is an hypothesis; some of these gods can be identified with those of certain of the races without much question, how far they all can remains yet to be studied.

30. The first group, the partly animal gods, which we should expect to be linked more or less with the negro element, are fourteen in number. Selk, the scorpion; Uazit and Nekhebt, the serpents of north and south; Hekt, the frog of birth; Horakhti, the hawk; Mentu, the hawk; Tahuti, the ibis; Sebek, the crocodile; Taurt, the hippopotamus; Hapi, the bull; Khnum, the ram; Un-nefer, the hare; Anpu or Apuat, the jackal; Sekhet or Bast, the lion. Each of these may appear in human form, with the head or some attribute of the animal, or at least standing and acting as a human being. In this they are distinct from the sacred animals. Apparently of this same stratum are the gods of the dead, Mertseger, the serpent of Thebes, and Seker of Sakkara, whose kingdom of the dead is older than that of Osiris, and whose form apart from other gods we do not know, unless it be that of the mummied hawk which broods over his sacred bark and shrine. With this stratum we may probably also link the *ka* and *ba*; their purely earthly existence and their dependence on the tree-spirit pointing to their early position.

31. The second group is distinguished by

being linked together in the mythology, and being in almost every case represented under purely human forms. Isis and her son Horus worshipped at Buto, and Osiris, afterwards united to her, are the principal and typical gods of this group. Set—the only animal-headed god of the group—is closely related to the great triad, first as the fellow-god of Horus, and later as the enemy of Osiris and Horus. The outline of the history of this change we have already noticed, and its significance as embodying a piece of tribal history. There is also the great Horus, or elder Horus, who appears to represent the heaven, the *her*, or upper region, and whose two eyes are the sun and moon. Very possibly he was one with the younger Horus originally, who became posed as a son of Isis in consequence of some tribal union requiring a fusion of the gods. Nebhat is the remaining divinity of this family, whom some regard as a mere interpolation to provide a wife to Set.

Another family of this same character is that of the Thebaid. Amen is a human god, and Mut and Khonsu are purely human in their figures. Anher is another god of the heaven, probably belonging to a different tribe from the Horus worshippers. Net or Neith, the great goddess of Sais, was likewise entirely human. All of these gods are figured as men and women, they have essentially human passions and action, and there is nothing mystic about them. That they form a different class to the first is seen by their duplication: worshippers of Tahuti had no need to invent a fresh god of the moon and of time, in Khonsu; those who went to Sokar had no need to invent Osiris as a god of the dead. The links of this class are all to the western races. Osiris was identified with the worship of the Dad emblem, lord of Daddu; and this appears connected with the south Libyan god Dadun. The Dionysiac character of Osiris is very strong, and Dionysos was reared in Libya. Osiris appears to be the god of vegetation, the corn god, which was a main deity of the white races. The oracular character of Amen and Khonsu is a western idea, and Amen was expressly the god of the great Oasis, and was worshipped in Laconia, Elis, and Bœotia. Neit has always been recognized as a Libyan goddess; and the very close connection of her nature (as the goddess of the lance or arrow, and also of

EGYPTIAN MYTHOLOGY

weaving) links her with Athena, who came from Libya. The Elysian theory of the soul is that belonging to this second group.

32. The next main group is that of the cosmic gods, of whom Ra is the chief. Beside the main figure of Ra there are the parallel gods Atmu, the sun before the world, ever-existing; Khepra, the present sun; and Harakhti, the rising sun. Of these Ra was the direct primitive god, and Harakhti a popular variant combined with the previous Horus worship; while Atmu and Khepra are more theological gods, never worshipped by the people. Nefer-atmu was a son of Atmu, who was hardly more than of local importance. Nut and Seb were the heaven and the earth, and Shu the air or space which separates them. In the earliest form it is Ra who separates them; but either form of the daily rising of Nut from Seb is evidently the lifting of the fog and mist of the Nile valley from off the earth and raising it up into the clouds of the sky. The sun does this by shining on it, so Ra separates Seb and Nut; while later the more abstract idea of space—Shu—was considered the separator. The ostrich feather, the hieroglyph of Shu, is

the most imponderable object for its bulk that could be selected, and hence the emblem of space. Tefnut is merely complementary to Shu. The moon-god Aah probably belongs to this group; and the other form of the sun—Aten—being worshipped in the centre of Ra influence, belongs to the same ideas.

These gods, though human in form, differ essentially from the previous group, as having all of them a cosmic meaning, and representing the elements of nature,—earth, sky, air, and sun. Their connection with the twelve hours is very marked; the sun was always passing through the hours of day or night, and every hour had a different nature and was the region of different spirits. The great seat of this worship was at Heliopolis; and that city—the abode of "the spirits of Heliopolis"—was a centre of literature and theology. In this we see a strong kinship to Mesopotamia; there the twelve hours ruled all divisions of time or space, the worship of spirits or demons was frequent, and great libraries were associated with the temples. Above all the cosmic view of religion predominated; the sun, moon, and stars were adored, and the watery chaos was parallel to the waters of Nu, while the waters above the heavens were parallel to the solar river of the Egyptians on which the bark of the sun was navigated. Of course, the solar theory of the soul was that associated with this religion. The Mesopotamian influence in Egypt has long been recognized, and is seen to be later than the Osirian. In this it agrees to the position of the Mesopotamians invading the Negro-Libyan population. And we should, perhaps, see in Heliopolis the centre of power of the Eastern invaders.

33. The fourth class of gods are those which embody more abstract ideas. Ptah the creator, who is neither Atmu the sun, nor Khnumu the modeller, but rather the architect of the universe, who puts it all into order, with his companion Maat, who is abstract truth and law. This is a very different view to that of any of the other gods. And similar in idealism is Min the all-father, and Hathor the all-mother. Later developments of these brought in Imhotep with Ptah, as a son representing the peace and learning which follows on law and order. And Hathor became linked with Isis, the previous mother goddess, though both are

still figured separately side by side in the XIXth Dynasty; and Horus thus came to be connected with the Min-worship. The general diffusion of Hathor-worship over all the country, without excluding any previous divinity, led to special Hathors of each nome, like the special Madonnas of different towns; and to Hathor being identified with many of the goddesses. It is not improbable that the system of mummifying belongs to this class of gods. We have noticed that it is independent of all the other theories of the soul, and was probably a later system; and the fact of the Hathor cow being represented as galloping into the unseen world bearing the mummy on her back, points to the mummification being part of the religion of Hathor. Historically we should see in this class of gods those of the latest prehistoric invaders, the Punite race. Min and Hathor we have already seen to belong to that quarter; and Ptah is the same as the Patekh of the Phœnicians, another branch of the Punites.

We must, however, carefully notice that this view of some group of gods having the same nature, and belonging to the same race, does not at all imply that they were originally worshipped together. They may very probably have belonged to different tribes; and only have been put side by side as tribal or political union spread. Min and Ptah may never have been worshipped together until their tribes entered Egypt. Amen and Osiris may have been strangers until their followers became unified in one land. All that we can venture to do is to outline a broad classification by general direction, east, west, or south, and gain some general idea of the sequence in time, without any hope as yet of separating between the various tribes of each quarter.

34. There now remain to be considered the gods which appear to be foreign, that is to say, which belong to invaders who did not exercise an influence over the whole country. One of the most important of these is Bes, the god of dancing, music, and luxury. The earliest of such figures are clearly female, and down to the latest age a female Bes appears as well as the male form. The shaggy lion's head is seen on a carving of the XIIth Dynasty to be a skin worn on the head, with the tail hanging down behind; and such a mask was imitated in cartonnage for the use of

dancers. How ancient professional dancers were in Egypt is seen in the Westcar papyrus, where the goddesses appear as travelling dancing girls. It seems then that Bes originates in the type of a girl wearing a lion's skin. It was considered Arabian in origin, but has been connected with the Denga or dwarf who is named as dancing a sacred dance in the Vth and VIth Dynasties. It seems hard not to connect this with the lion-headed goddess of the Arabian nome, Best or Bast, especially as dancing festivals were held in her honour.

The distinctly Syrian deities are six: Anaitis, Astarte, Baal, Kedesh, Reshpu, and Sutekh; and the worship of these belongs to the great age of Syrian mixture, the XVIIIth and XIXth Dynasties.

35. It remains now to notice how much the worship of many of these gods fluctuates, how one god would sink, while others rose in importance. We can best see this statistically by the number of references to gods in various periods; but we must first set aside those which rose in one age without any previous popularity, such as Amen. Fixing our attention on the principal gods worshipped throughout all ages, and reducing

EGYPTIAN MYTHOLOGY

the numbers so as to give them a percentage in each period, we have the following results:

	IVth Dynasty.	Vth Dynasty.	VIth Dynasty.	XIIth Dynasty.	XVIII.–Am. III.	Am.IV.–XX.
Hekt	—	1	2	5	—	1
Tahuti	23	21	17	10	7	9
Khnumu	1	—	—	17	1	—
Anpu	—	3	2	—	4	5
Sokar	10	13	14	—	1	2
Osiris	5	—	2	12	8	12
Isis	1	—	2	2	9	12
Horus	10	10	5	7	18	15
Neit	8	7	5	7	1	2
Ra	1	1	5	2	26	14
Seb	1	—	2	—	5	2
Ptah	9	2	13	2	1	8
Maat	1	8	5	—	3	5
Min	5	5	5	12	1	4
Hathor	25	29	21	24	15	9

Here we can see how the Osiride and Cosmic gods rose in importance as time went on, while the Abstract gods continually sank on the whole. This agrees to the general idea that the later imported gods have to yield their position gradually to the older and more deeply-rooted faiths.

LECTURE V.

THE NATURE OF CONSCIENCE

36. IT has long been recognized that the Egyptians had a much more highly organized conscience than that of most other nations of early times. They are often spoken of as a more moral people; but that phrase is ambiguous, as it may refer to the complexity of the conscience, or the practical conformity to the conscience. How far the Egyptians conformed to their theoretic standards is quite a different question; but their standards were certainly more definite, and apparently higher, than those of many other peoples. In many respects they are far higher than those of the Greeks, and approach most to the Roman standard after Stoic philosophy and Christianity had successively purged and improved it. This organized conscience has left many detailed expositions to us, in the Precepts of Kagemni

THE NATURE OF CONSCIENCE

and Ptahhotep of the Vth Dynasty; in the two negative confessions or repudiations of sins before the judgment of Osiris, which are probably much older, but only exist in later versions; in the tablet of Antef of the XIIth Dynasty (Brit. Mus., Sharpe, ii. 83); Instructions of Amenemhat of the XIIth Dynasty; in the maxims of Any of the XIXth Dynasty; the precepts in a Ptolemaic papyrus in the Louvre (x. 9), and isolated sayings in the XIth Dynasty Song of the Harper, and some grave steles. We are, therefore, able to study it in detail, and to classify a mass of ideas which have definite dates affixed to them as a minimum; hence we obtain a tolerably complete view of the Conscience of the Egyptians. One great value of such a study is that it is dealing with a people so much more advanced than their neighbours in such ideas, that we have before us an internally developing system rather than an accidental jumble of imposed ideas from other sources, which constitutes the morality of most later races.

37. It may not be out of place to consider first, somewhat briefly, what we mean by conscience: not by any means to construct an artificial definition of the idea, nor to

argue as to its limits in relation to other conceptions, for that would lead us into the barren grounds of speculation. But rather let us look practically at the acts of others around us, and into own our minds. Conscience is that mass of the intuitions of right and wrong, which are born in the structure of the thoughts, though they may often need development before the latent structure becomes active. A plant does not put out its leaves and flowers all at once; yet they are latent, and are inevitable if any development of growth takes place. And thus, perhaps, some can look back to a time when only one or two elements of conscience were yet active in their minds, such as a sense of justice and injustice, and they reflected then that no act would seem wrong or shocking if it was not unjust. Yet later on, as the mind grew (and growth or death is the choice to the mind, though the body may continue an animal existence), the various other elements of conscience unfolded gradually from some central stem (such as that of justice) which had first sprung up.

It is needful to remember thus that conscience is an inherited development, as much

THE NATURE OF CONSCIENCE 89

an inheritance in the structure of the brain as any other special modification is in the body—needful because in the consideration of the springs of action it has been generally the habit to deal with the individual as if he had a perfectly blank mind, and was only impressed by the facts of life around him in a perfectly calculating and unbiassed manner. On the contrary the untrained mind teems with prospects of every kind, possible and impossible, at every change of surrounding, and acts far more by impulse and intuition than by precise calculations of theoretical right or utility. This is seen most plainly in the waywardness of children and savages; the ideas of all kinds of possibilities are present, and the growth of conscience and of habit is not yet strong enough to determine uniformly which opening shall be followed. Thus we may look on each person as only a fragment of the common life of mankind, inheriting in his brain-structure a tendency to certain lines of action and certain choices between opposing claims. He is the heir of all his ancestors, and specially of those nearest to him; for, as Galton has shown by physical tests, inheritance of special characters rapidly diminishes in each succeeding generation, and there is a constant tendency thus to revert to an average type.

38. From this point of view we see at once how it is that the utilitarian—such as Mill or Herbert Spencer—can point triumphantly to the fact that the moral ideas of right conform to what is the greatest utility, though often a far-fetched utility to the race, rather than utility directly to the individual. It is not, as he assumes, that the individual argues carefully from utility to right; but, rather, that the stress of utility has throughout human history crushed out all those strains of thought that were least helpful. Starting with the wild mass of wayward minds with infinitely varying choice of action before each, all those which were least useful in the long run went to the wall, found difficulties and hindrances to life prevail against them, and died out. Those minds whose impulses were the most useful and most regular and consistent succeeded best, and hence that type of brain descended to future generations. In short, utility has been the great selecting agent in brain variation as in bodily variation. And the result is that the great mass of inherited habits of thought, which we call intuitions or conscience, are

those which in the long run are most useful to the individual and to his community in general; those which will lead his descendants most surely to success among their fellows, and which will help his community to hold its ground against others. Here we have a complete explanation of the often distant and intricate utility of some intuition or moral principle, which may be directly opposed to the comfort or even the well-being of the individual. A mental type of a community which produces on the average a certain number of martyrs to conscience, may thus ensure to itself that strength which may lead it to success over the fallen bodies of its saviours; their conduct is strictly utilitarian, though it would be impossible to deduce it from any argument of utility to themselves. I have dwelt on this because it constrains us in the most decisive way to place utility as the blind selecting agent acting on the race, and not as the choice of the individual, and so explains the utilitarian action of the person apart from any argument in his own mind. (See Note A.)

This clears out of the way the imperious, yet sole, argument against the reality of the rule of intuition; and we are free to accept what is to some—perhaps to all—the obvious mode of working of the mind. We do not act by elaborate calculation of consequences, but by a certain sense of what seems the inevitable course in the circumstances; we follow our inherited intuitions, and the more we develop and unfold them, the more we let them rule over the mere impulse of the momentary feeling, the safer we are and the more surely are we in the way of right fulfilment. We are, then, trusting not to momentary expediency, but to the great growth of intuition, battered and lopped and toughened into its most sturdy and useful form by all the blasts of adversity that countless ancestors have endured, and by which they have been shaped. This is Conscience.

In thus briefly glancing over the ground, as a mere explanatory preface to our view of Conscience among the Egyptians, we cannot possibly deal with the various constructive evidences by which we are led to this general statement: such as the examples of hereditary intuition and mental processes, apart from education; the parallels of physical inheritance; the manifest growth of a body of moral intuition, even in the midst of decaying societies where everything was against each fresh generation; the absence of conscience in most races where early marriage prevails; and the well-known advantage of the later over the earlier members of the same family in their mental ability, tact, and intuition, due to their inheriting a more developed brain. But we have here indicated that such a view of the conscience, as a body of intuition gradually shaped by the stress of hard utility, and pruned of all its varieties that were not permanently successful,—that such a view is the key which fits the great puzzle of the strength of intuition and the prevalence of utility, as no other explanation can fit it.

39. This leads to the practical view of the paramount value of the proper unfolding of the inherited intuitions, and of the strengthening, selecting, and guarding of them by each person who is thus the temporary trustee of the great inheritance of the race. A duty to this precious growth which is paramount over all other duties of life to the person, to the fellow-men to whom the individual's character is the most valued part of him, and to those who may come after. A rightly organ-

ized intuition of moral perception, of judgment, and of feeling, is worth any amount of temporizing calculations, which always have to deal with unknown forces. And this is indeed most closely parallel to our acquisition of knowledge in other matters. Probably few, if any, persons remember even a small part of what they read; and yet there is all the difference possible between a well-read and an ignorant man. In what does this difference consist if the actual words and facts are not remembered? It consists in the education of his intuitive knowledge, in shaping and leading the mind, so that without being able to quote a single exact parallel, he can yet frame a correct judgment on history or on present life, and say at once if an assertion is likely or a future event is probable. Often a book is read—perhaps most books are read—not to retain a single detail in mind, but in order to consciously modify or expand the general mass of opinion and knowledge in the mind. And this is one of the strongest revelations to us of the vast mass of organized intuitions which we unconsciously bear in our minds, to which we apply on all occasions, and by which we rule our lives.

40. To most people the ideas of varieties of right and wrong are but vague; some things are judged to be always right, others always wrong, and many between are said to "depend upon circumstances." The whole subject seems indefinable; a sort of mist, with some kind of a heaven at the top, and some kind of a hell at the bottom of it. And often there is a vague notion that many things are right according to one code, and wrong according to another; a difference formulated in the discrepancies between custom, law, and canon law.

Yet amid all this there is a general agreement as to the relative scale of right and wrong actions in any one subject, and most people will agree that one action is certainly better or worse than another. The confusion mainly comes in when we attempt to pit a right of one kind against a wrong of another kind, as when we attempt to weigh kindness against injustice.

Now if we can bring in any system of thought in order to arrange our ideas on this it will be a great gain. Not an arbitrary regulation, nor a code of abstract notions, nor any *a priori* arguments; of such there have been far too many. What we need to do is to ascertain what the actual ways of human thoughts really are, and to what laws they conform. The only way to begin is to view one subject at a time, such as truthfulness, kindness, self-restraint, or justice. Of these it will be most convenient to take truthfulness as the example for discussion; and one particular branch of that, as exhibited in honesty towards the government, is what we can learn more about than any other.

The first thing to arrange our ideas about is the relative order in which most men regard degrees of truthfulness. Let us lay down certain stages of falsehood which may be generally regarded as clearly each worse than the previous.

Lying to save many innocent lives,
„ to save one innocent life,
„ to save great losses of property or character to others,
„ to save great pain to others,
„ to avoid great pain,
„ to save family character,
„ to gain advantage for a family,
„ to save personal character,
„ to gain important personal advantage,
„ for moderate gain,
„ for pleasures,

Lying for sake of contradictions,
",, for trivial gain,
",, to annoy others,
",, to avoid slight pain or inconvenience,
",, for pleasure of deception,
",, from hatred of anything going aright.

Here we should have something like a definite scale of one particular virtue, always supposing that the directness of the lie was equal, say a plain direct negative to a direct question clearly expected. Of course many people would descend to a far lower level if a mere suggestion or innuendo would gain their end. Now this is not a mere curiosity, or piece of casuistry, to form such a scale; it is like the earliest thermometers, divided into "temperate," "summer heat," "blood heat," and "fever heat," it is the first step to definition. What point in the scale some ancient Greeks would have occupied may be seen in Note B.

41. The next step is to consider how many people will descend to each of these levels. Out of a hundred ordinary people perhaps only one would refuse to tell a lie to save a man's life; perhaps twenty or thirty might be truthful in face of great pain of mind or body; perhaps fifty would be

truthful where no great advantage was to be gained; perhaps eighty would resist the temptation where only small gains or spite was the reason; and only one or two would lie out of sheer perversity.

The common idea probably is that a large part of our race are to be classed as "truthful," all much alike, and below that there are fewer and fewer truthful folks found in increasing "depths of depravity." Perhaps those who would be reckoned usually as truthful are people who would not lie to save themselves great pain, or to save the characters of their family. If we then call attention to higher degrees of truthfulness they are merely said to be "exceptional."

In short, if we were to represent each person who descended to a particular level by a stroke, |, we should have so many strokes above one level, so many more who descended lower, so many more who descended lower still, and so forth, until we could define the proportion of people who are included in each successive stage of

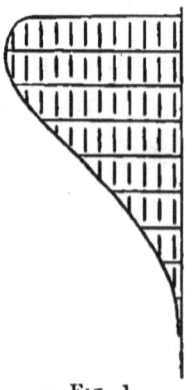

FIG. 1.

THE NATURE OF CONSCIENCE

truthfulness by an outline as here shown. (Fig. 1.)

But we have no right to draw a line anywhere as the abstract truthfulness; the higher grades are just as much part of the whole series as the lower; and if it is true that very few persons will limit themselves by the highest grades, so it is also true that very few descend to the lowest. The extreme cases are the exceptions, and we may mark them by a single example; on the other hand, there is a great mass of mankind about the middle grades, and we must, therefore, have a great many strokes there (Fig. 2); the outline then that defines the commonness of different grades of lying will be widest out in the middle, and run off tapering above and below.

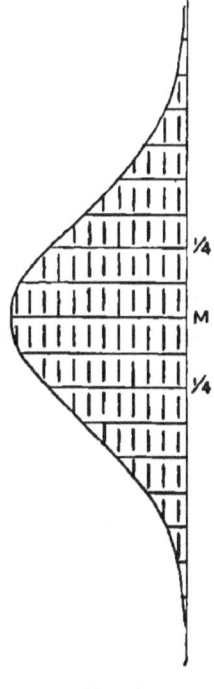

FIG. 2.

Now this approximates to the result which is very well known as the law of distribution of errors, or the "probability curve." That is to say, that whenever a simple quality is liable to variation, whether it be the height or weight of a large number of men or animals, the variations of temperature, the errors of measurement, or any other simple variable, it is always found that the greater part of the examples are in the middle, and fewer toward the ends; and that if, for instance, a certain number of men vary one inch from the average height, there will be a fixed proportion that vary two inches, and another fixed proportion that vary three inches, and so forth. So that the distribution of variation, or the number of examples that agree to each different standard, always follows a certain law of distribution. So certain is this that any distinct departure from this distribution is always accepted as proof that some disturbing cause is at work; a different kind of distribution would be found for instance in the height of soldiers, because all men below a certain standard are rejected.

Is it possible then that moral distribution follows the same law as all other natural variations? To anyone accustomed to the regularity of the distribution of all other variations, this would hardly seem to need proof. But to many persons moral law is supposed to be something so spiritual, and so outside of the realm of force and matter, that it may be surprising to see it treated

THE NATURE OF CONSCIENCE 101

like any other case of the variations found in nature. It is difficult to obtain any sufficient mass of accurate information on any subject of morals or conscience for us to test exactly this general similarity that we have seen to probably hold good between moral and physical distribution.

42. One subject, however, promises to give a result. The well-known contributions of "Conscience Money" to the Exchequer afford a large mass of statistics, and I have dealt with nearly five thousand amounts received during thirty years, the details of which I was permitted to have extracted from the Treasury records. It is true that this only refers to a section of the population, those who happen to escape paying their legal assessment, and who yet feel uneasy at not having done so. From certain details that we can observe, it appears that these payments are largely the sums of continued accumulations of arrears, rather than single large items; and this is all the better for our purpose, as the amounts thus represent what *strains the conscience* in different individuals and makes them uneasy enough to take the trouble, and make up their minds, to give up the amount due to

the Exchequer. This is also an admirable subject for study from the comparative simplicity of the motives involved. There is no influence of affection nor of shame, as the payment is made to the impersonal nation at large, and is very generally anonymous, and never the subject of self-advertisement or glorification. We cannot say as much for any other form of payment depending on the conscience. Moreover, it covers all classes of society except the very lowest, and varies as much as one to a million in its effects.

When we come to treat the amounts thus received we find that they follow very closely indeed the general law of the distribution of variations. The main exception is the deficiency from about £1 10s. to £5, and the great excess at £5. This is readily accounted for by the fact that so many payments are anonymous, and a £5 note is one of the handiest ways of making anonymous payments. That this facility of the £5 note abstracts from the proportion of lower payments is interesting evidence that the payments are cumulative amounts and not mostly single dues. The man who owes over 30/- or so is induced to hold back until

THE NATURE OF CONSCIENCE 103

he can send the convenient £5 note. The many other results we cannot treat of at present, but will only say that the more punctilious conscience belongs to rather poorer people whose average is only £2 or £3 due, and not £5 16s., which is the usual average due; that conscience is twice as keen in March as it is in September, the economy of the winter enabling men to afford a conscience better than when anticipating or enjoying the summer holiday; and the clearing of conscience is largely a vague affair of a round lump sum, not half the payments being at all exact amounts.

The most important result, however, is that conscience is, like all other variables, subject to the laws of averages and distribution. That exactly as many people will pay in a tenth of the average amount as pay in ten times the average, as many payments of 10/- as there are of £50; or further, as many people will pay in 1/6 or $\frac{1}{64}$ of the average as pay in £320 or 64 times the average. This distinctive point of the law of probabilities, the equality of instances at points equidistant from the average, above and below it, is fully and remarkably carried out, though we here deal with conscience concerning pence on the one hand and hundreds of pounds on the other. For some further details see Note C.

43. Having thus obtained one of the best

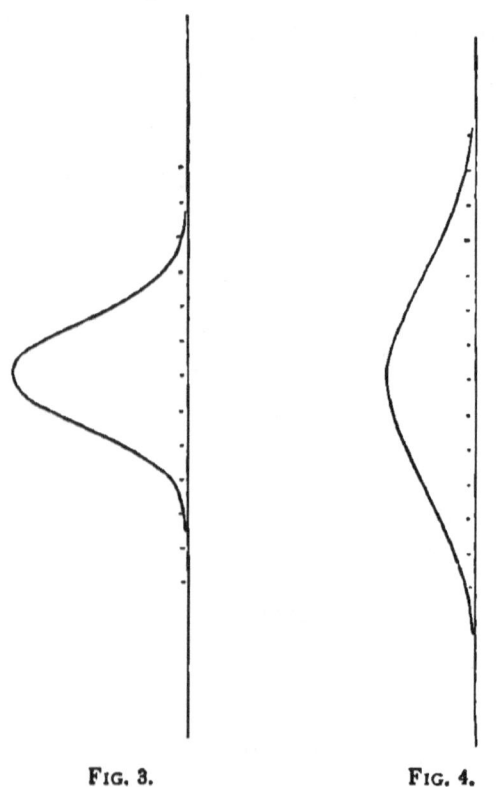

Fig. 3.   Fig. 4.

and most unmixed confirmations that we can hope to get of the application of the laws of distribution to moral questions, let us apply this system as a mode of visualizing and giving consistency to our thoughts on such subjects. We may say in looking at such a curve that it represents the variations of mood and influences in the individual which determine his good and bad acts; or the variations between individuals in a whole class or nation. We can contrast rigid and narrow habits (Fig. 3) with those of wider feeling and passion (Fig. 4). We can represent the character of the morality of different men or different races (Fig. 5) — some (A) very variable and reaching great heights as well as great depths — some (B) rather high as a whole, but not varying so much and never so good or so bad as A; some (C) very uniform, but never worth much.

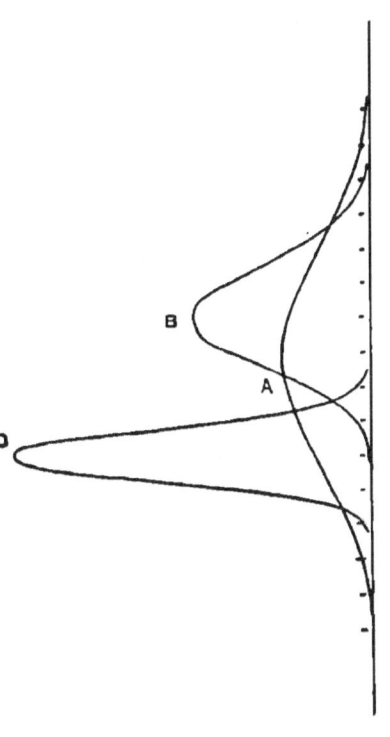

FIG. 5.

And further, this enables us to clearly think of the effects which a standard of conduct may have on the national conscience. Many people will be affected by the existence of a standard; those who are naturally a little worse than the standard will be considerably drawn to conform to it; those who are more distant from it will less often feel it possible to pay attention to it; and those who are very far below it will not even try

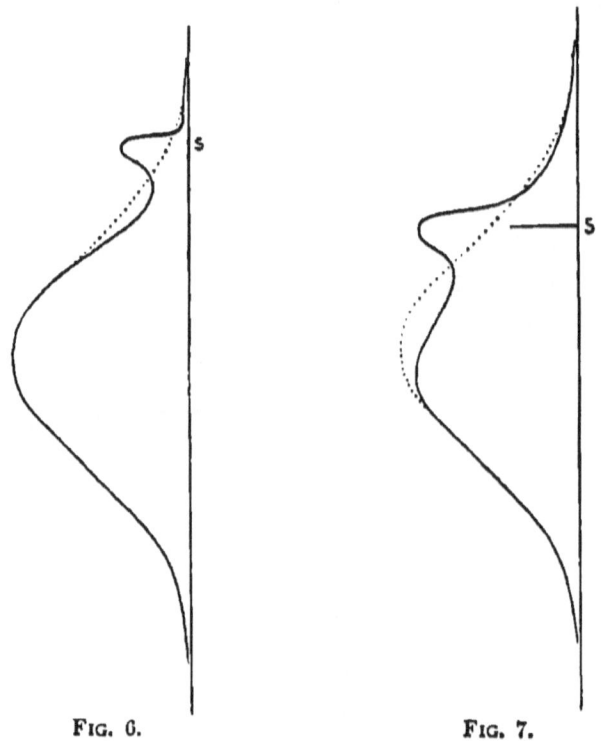

Fig. 6.   Fig. 7.

to regard it. Also those who would otherwise be a little better than the standard will give way and say that it is good enough for them, while those far above it will hold to their own high level.

44. This brings before us very forcibly

THE NATURE OF CONSCIENCE 107

the question of the benefit of a very high standard, or one nearer the common average. In the case of a very high standard the danger is that it will attract such a slender portion of the whole area of variation that it will benefit very few people (Fig. 6); and, in short, be hypocritically concurred in, but practically disregarded. A standard nearer to the average will have a more generally useful effect (Fig. 7); while one even lower may yet be more useful, as in Fig. 8. But too low a standard may do no good by not being far enough from the average to raise it. Of course, the stronger the standard, or the greater influence there is of religion, shame, good feeling, or other motive for obeying it, the further it may be placed from the average, while yet having sufficient attractive power to be of value in its results.

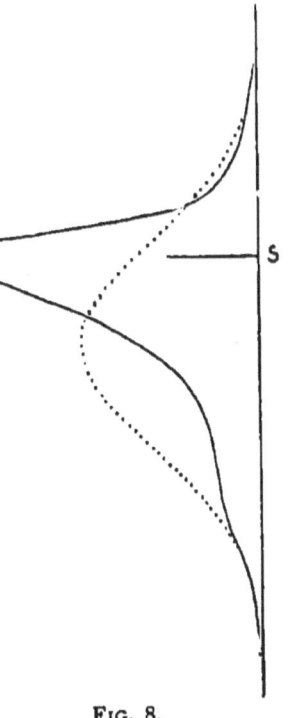

Fig. 8.

There may be also two or three different

standards all acting at once (Fig. 9); a very high church-going standard, very seldom effective; a powerful lower standard of trade custom; and a residuum much lower than that, of the natural character.

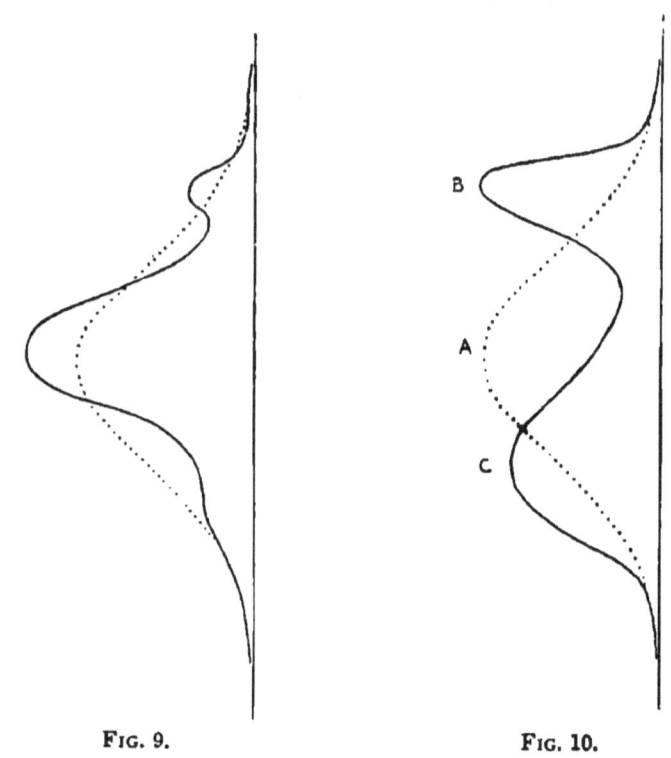

Fig. 9.   Fig. 10.

And two or three standards may co-exist in one character owing to antagonistic motives, which result in a course of action which is often in extremes (Fig. 10). For instance, on a basis of general good nature (A) a man may have a strong family affection (B), but be extremely avaricious (C). When he comes to dealing with his children he may be therefore in money matters readily in extremes, but not so often in a middle course.

We have at least now seen enough to be able to picture before us the variations of motive and character; and we can thus consider the nature of conscience with a mental analysis and a clearness of conception which would otherwise be impossible.

LECTURE VI.

THE INNER DUTIES

45. In dealing with nearly two hundred maxims or expressions of conscience which we have gathered from Egyptian sources, it is needful to have some system of classifying them, so as to place together those which are similar and which serve together to build up a picture of the Egyptian mind on one side or another. Seven classes are here separately dealt with, namely, the rules and maxims of (1) the personal character; (2), the material interests; (3), the family duties, all of which we may call the *inner duties;* while the *outer duties* are (4) the relations to equals; (5), the relations to superiors; (6), the relations to inferiors; (7), the duties to the gods. And in each class we shall deal with the general ideas before noticing the more particular and detailed. For most of the translations here

I am indebted to Mr. Griffith, who feels considerable reserve about some of the renderings. The tablet of Antef is from a copy made by Mr. Alan Gardiner.

46. One of the most valuable sources of our information is in the (5) great "negative confession" as it is commonly called, or rather "repudiation of sins" as it might be better termed, before the judgment of Osiris. It is probably one of the oldest documents that remain to us on this subject, and is specially valuable, as it presumably strings together every action that was felt to be an infringement of moral law at the time when it was composed. There are two forms of this repudiation; one of about 37 declarations, and another, similar in nature, often repeating the earlier list, but of 42 declarations. The latter is more artificial, as it calls on a separate spirit in each declaration; and the number 42 is probably connected with the 42 judges who sit with Osiris, and those, in turn, with the division of Egypt into 42 nomes.

It is strange that there are no family duties in either declaration; and this suggests that the bond of the family was not of prominent importance at the time of the framing of these lists, but that such duties were considered only as a part of the general duties to fellow-beings. Of the classes of duties then we find—

	List A.	List B.
Duties to character	7	18
Duties to material welfare	0	0
Duties to family	0	0
Duties to equals	13	16
Duties to inferiors	10	1
Duties to superiors	0	0
Duties to gods	9	6

The main difference between these two lists is that in the earlier time the duties to inferiors were put more forward than the duties to the man's own character; in the later time the duty to the development of character and of intuitions was felt to include in it all that was needful to recount as duty to inferiors. The two lists are simply referred to as A and B hereafter.

47. The Egyptian felt very strongly the value of strength of character, and of self-control. "I have not been weak," he boldly asserted to Osiris (A. 10) as one of the repudiations of wrong-doing, which qualified him for eternal blessing. And Any says,

"Let not the heart despair before thyself, turning upside down its favours (happiness)* at once after an evil hour" (60); this large-minded steadfastness is also enjoined by Any thus, "If thou art good thou shalt be regarded; and in company or in solitude thou findest thy people (helpers) and they do all thy commands." (34.) And similarly Any enjoins firm resolutions, "If thou goest in the straight road, thou shalt reach the intended place" (Any, 29); and also "Give thine eye (look well to thyself); thy existence lowly or lofty is not well fixed (is liable to change); go straight forward, and thou wilt fill the way." (Any, 44.) There will be no room for deviation and uncertainty if a resolute course is firmly adopted.

Of self-training and control we read, "If thou art found good in the time of prosperity, when adversity comes thou wilt find thyself able to endure." (Any, 32.) And again, "Be not greedy to fill thy stomach, for one knows no reason why he should do so; when thou camest into existence I gave thee a different excellency." (Any, 42.) Or to put this in

---

* The words and phrases in parentheses are paraphrases, additions, or alternative expressions to show the meaning more clearly, while not modifying the actual idiom of the original.

western words, "Yield not to mere desires which rest not upon reason, for you were made for better things than that."

Self-respect is also enjoined by Any: "If a man is drunken, go not before him, even when it would be an honour to be introduced" (6); and also, "Go not among the multitude, in order that thy name may not be fouled." (9.) And in the later precepts it is said, "Make not a companion of a wicked man." (3.)

Readiness and boldness appear in the early time of Ptah-hotep: "If thou findest a debater in his moment (speaking successfully) thine equal, who is within thy reach, to whom thou canst cause thyself to become superior, be not silent when he speaketh evil; a great thing is the approval of the hearers, that thy name should be good in the knowledge of the nobles." (3.) And later Any says similarly, "He who is embarrassed by a liar should make reply; then god judgeth truly, and his trespass riseth against him." (38.)

Activity was also one of the great claims for the future blessing: before Osiris the soul declared, "I have not been lazy" (B. 11), and "I have not been empty (of good)." (A. 9.) And similarly, "I have

THE INNER DUTIES

not known vanity (meanness or unprofitableness)" (A. 4); and "I have not made bubbles." (B 39.) Special importance to straightforwardness was also given in the declaration at the judgment. "I have not acted perversely instead of straightforwardly." (A. 3.) "I have not acted crookedly" (B. 7); "I have not made confusion" (B. 25); "I have not been deaf to the words of truth." (B. 24.) Thus no less than eight declarations in the most solemn list of the great judgment turn on the activity and directness of character, which has in all ages been a quality worth even more than the cleverness of subtlety.

A delightful picture is drawn by Ptahhotep of the disastrous lack of common sense, that is as well known now as in his early times. "Verily the ignorant man who hearkeneth not, nothing can be done to him. He seeth knowledge as ignorance; profitable things as hurtful; he maketh every kind of mistake so that he is reprimanded every day. His life is as death therewith; it is his food. Absurdity of talk he marvelleth at as the knowledge of nobles, dying while he liveth every day. People avoid having to do with him, on account of the multitude of his continual misfortunes." (Ptah-hotep, 40.) And this avoidance of fools appears again in the late precept "Go not out with a foolish man, nor stop to listen to his words" (Precepts, 21, 22), and "Do not according to the advice of a fool." (Precept 4.)

48. But, perhaps, greater stress is laid upon discretion and quietness than on any other qualities of character. It is remarkable that it does not occur at all in the earlier repudiation of sins, but is very prominent in the later; in that we find, " My mouth hath not run on" (B. 17): " My mouth hath not been hot" (B. 23); " I have not quarrelled" (B. 29); " My voice has not been voluble in my speech" (B. 33); and " My voice is not loud." (B. 37.) Here five out of the forty pleas of goodness turn on a single quality, which would hardly appear at all in a board-school code of morals. Yet such are the virtues requisite for the blessed fields of Aalu in the kingdom of Osiris. This same discreetness is urged by old Ptah-hotep, "Let thy heart be overflowing, but let thy mouth be restrained: consider how thou shalt behave among the nobles. Be exact in practice with thy master; act so that he shall say, 'The son of that man shall

THE INNER DUTIES

speak to those that shall hearken; praiseworthy also is he who formed him.' Apply thine heart while thou art speaking, that thou mayest speak things of distinction; then the nobles who shall hear will say, 'How good is that which proceedeth out of his mouth.'" (Ptah-hotep, 42.) Later on Antef says, "I am one who is cool, free of hastiness of countenance, knowing results." (2.) And Any also has several injunctions to the same quietness. "Seek silence for thee." (Any, 62.) "Go not into the crowd if thou findest thyself excited in the presence of violence." (Any, 49.) "Of what shouldest thou talk daily? Let officials talk of their affairs, a woman talk of her husband, and every man talk of his business." (Any, 30.) And in more detail he says, "If there is enquiry, increase not thy words; in keeping quiet thou wilt do best; do not be a talker" (Any, 10); and again, "Guard thyself from sinning in words, that they may not wound; a thing to be condemned in the breast of man is malicious gossip, which is never still. Discard the man who errs (thus) and let him not be thy companion." (Any, 16.) And the repudiation of sins also brings in the condemnation of gossip. "I have not been a tale-bearer in business not mine own." (B. 18.)

Extreme reserve is inculcated by some writers. Kagemni says, "The cautious man succeeds, the accurate man is praised, to the man of silence (even) the sleeping chamber is opened. Wide scope hath he who is acquiescent in his speech; knives are set against him who forceth his way wrongfully." (Kagemni 1.) Amenemhat bitterly remarks as a precept for the highest station, "Mankind turn their heart to him who inspireth them with fear: fill not thy heart with a brother" (Am. ii.); and again, "Keep to thyself thy own heart, for friends exist not for a man on the day of troubles." (Am. iii.) Such cynical reserve was not, however, the Egyptian ideal, but it was what they preferred at least to weak gossip.

Covetousness is named in the repudiation of sins. "I have not been covetous" (B. 3.); and this is put in a more concrete form by Any, "Fill not thy heart with the things of another; beware of this. For thy own sake go not near the things of another, unless he shows them himself in thy house." (Any, 24.)

The evil of presumption and pride was

met by remarks on the uncertainty of life. Kagemni says: " Let not thy heart be proud for valour in the midst of thy troops. Beware of overbearingness, for one knoweth not what shall happen, or what a god will do when he striketh." (Kagemni, 5.) And similarly Ptah-hotep begins : " Let not thy heart be great because of thy knowledge, but converse with the ignorant as with the learned ; for the limit of skill is not attainable, and there is no expert who is completely provided with what is profitable to him. Good speech is more hidden than are the precious stones sought for by female slaves amid the pebbles." (Ptah-hotep, 1.) And more picturesquely does Any remark on the ever changing nature of things. "The water-courses shifted in past years, and will yet again the next year. The large pools dry up, and their shores become deep cracks. Nothing comes to man alike. This is the reply of the Mistress of Life." (Any, 43.) And the steadfast unwavering mind that these reflections should enlarge is held up as a heavenly requisite in the repudiation of sins, where the soul asserts " I have not given way to anxious care" (A. 8); and " I am not of inconstant mind" (B. 31); and again, similarly, "I have not been wretched." (A. 11.)

49. But beside all these fortifying maxims the Egyptians had a keen idea, sometimes coming to the surface, that virtue was not entirely its own reward, and not solely an end in itself; but that the end of right conduct was right enjoyment. Ptah-hotep inculcated this: "He who doth accounts all day long hath not a pleasant moment; and yet he who enjoyeth himself all day long doth not provide for his house. The archer hitteth his mark, and so doth he who steereth, by letting it alone at one time and pulling at another. He that obeyeth his heart shall command." (Ptah-hotep, 25*a*.) And again, "Follow thy heart the time that thou hast; do not more than is commanded. Diminish not the time of following the heart, for that is abomination to the *ka** that its moment (opportunity of action) should be disregarded. Spend not the time of each day beyond what is needful for providing for thy house. When possessions are obtained follow the heart, for possessions

---

* For the consideration of the nature of the *ka*, as shown here, see Note D.

are not made of full use if (thou art) weary." (Ptah-hotep, 10.) And the song of the harper more freely enjoins: "Follow thy heart so long as thou existest . . . enjoy thyself beyond measure, let not thy heart faint, follow thy desire and thy happiness while thou art on earth." Such doctrine naturally led too far, as when a man in Ptolemaic times ingeniously places in his deceased wife's mouth on her tombstone the commands: "Enjoy the love of women and make holiday. . . . Thy desire to drink and to eat hath not ceased, therefore be drunken." But occasional intoxication does not seem to have been looked on very seriously, perhaps, just because it was so very occasional; in the tomb of Paheri (XVIIIth Dynasty) one lady at the party says: "Give me some wine for I am as dry as a straw"; and another, approving its quality, adds, "I should like to drink to intoxication."

50. We may then sum up the personal character which the Egyptian strove for, and even considered in many points to be essential for those who would enter into the kingdom of Osiris. He should be strong, steadfast, and self-respecting; active and

straightforward; quiet and discreet; and avoid covetousness and presumption. Yet with all this, while striving for the highest character, he was to keep the use of life before him and to avoid miserliness or asceticism. Other qualities which we value we shall notice in the relations to other men and to property; but so far as the solely personal qualities go this picture of the Egyptian mind is as fine a basis of the principles of character as has been laid down by any people. But yet we do not find any trace in it of the idea of sin, which was so familiar to the Hindus in early times; the Egyptian is the rather akin to the Greek mind, which sought out a fair and noble life without introspection or self-reproach. Yet the more personal sense is seen in India even as early as the Rig Veda, where in the hymns to Varuna (Ouranos) contemporary with the XVIIIth Egyptian Dynasty, or earlier, the Hindu said: "O Varuna! deliver us from the sins of our fathers. Deliver us from the sins committed in our persons . . . all this sin is not wilfully committed by us. Error or wine, anger or dice, or even thoughtlessness, has begotten sin. Even an elder brother leads his younger

THE INNER DUTIES 123

astray, sin is begotten even in our dreams."*
And soon after, between the XIXth and
XXIst Egyptian Dynasties, we read the
Hindu saying: "When confessed the sin
becomes less, since it becomes truth."†
Such ideas, however familiar to us, to whom
they have descended by way of Palestine,
are, however, quite foreign to the Mediter-
ranean conscience met with in Egypt and
in Greece; they belong essentially to the
ascetic mind that found no place in the
compact and practical frame of the ex-
cellencies of the early Egyptian, which so
closely resembles the character of the best
of the modern Egyptians.

MATERIAL WELFARE

51. Beside the maxims of entirely personal character there is a body of injunctions
relating to the more material welfare and
conduct which may be considered as a separate class. Self-help is enjoined by Ptah-
hotep: "If thou ploughest labour steadily
in the field, that god may make it great in
thy hand. Let not thy mouth be filled at

---

* *Rig Veda* vii. 89.
† *Satapatha Brahmana* ii. 5, 2, 20.

thy neighbour's table. . . . Verily he who possesseth prudence is as the possessor of good, he holdeth like a crocodile from the officials. (He does not get into trouble and have to give bribes.) Beg not as a poor man from him who is without children, and make no boast to him; the father is important even when the mother that beareth is wanting, for another woman may be added to her" (reckon not on inheriting from a childless man, for he may take another wife). (Ptah-hotep, 9.)

Prudence is enjoined by Any thus: "Keep thine eye open for fear that thou shalt go begging: there is no man, if he be often lazy (that shall escape want)" (Any, 21), and seizing opportunities also,—"If the hour be past, one seeks to save another." (Any, 4.)

Reserve and not trusting to others appear also in Any's sayings, "Give not over-much freedom to a man in thy house. When thou comest in and thou hearest of his presence, thou art saluted by his mouth, thou art told of his purpose and talking is done" (Any, 45); and in the bitter saying, "Thy entering into a village begins with acclamations; at thy going out thou art saved by thy hand." (Any, 64.)

A curious piece of worldly wisdom lies in the advice to imitate successful men. "If thou failest, follow a successful man; let all thy conduct be good before god. When thou knowest that a small man hath advanced, let not thine heart be proud toward him by reason of what thou knowest of him; to a man who hath advanced be respectful in proportion to what hath arrived to him, for behold things do not come of themselves, it is their law for those whom they love. Verily he who hath risen he hath been prudent for himself; it is god that maketh his success, and he would punish him if he were indolent." (Ptah-hotep, 10.) "Always do business with lucky people," is a well-known modern maxim.

Of the value of knowledge, above the power of connections and influence, Any speaks thus: "If thou art able in the writings, having penetrated into the writings, put them in thy heart, then all that thou sayest will be perfected. If a scribe is employed in any profession he speaks according to the writings (Precedents!). There is no son to the chief of the treasury, there is no heir to the chief of the seal (such officer must be fitted by ability and not by influence). The great appreciate the scribe, and his hand is his profession and cannot be given to children; their misery (of the great) is his good, their greatness is his protection." (35.) It is familiar to us how true this last sentence is of our scribes, the lawyers. But to feel the force of this let us turn to a community in which the scribe is in full sway. Writing of Emin Pasha's officials, Mr. Jephson says, "These soldiers were so foolish; again and again they found themselves tricked by the clerks. . . . The Egyptian clerks held the whole of these ignorant Sudani officers and men in their hands; they wrote all sorts of things, to which the Sudanis, who could neither read nor write, put their seals."

A conciliatory and peaceable manner was much valued; but all the injunctions come from Any in the XIXth Dynasty, and none from earlier times. "As the inside of man is like a granary, full of all kinds of replies, choose to thee the good, speak well, as there is abomination within thee. To reply violently is as lifting a stick. But speak with the sweetness of a lover. . . ." (37.) "One doth not get good things when one saith evil things." (28.) "Lift not up thy heart over

THE INNER DUTIES

the dissipated man so that he can find speech (against thee). The statements of thy mouth go round quickly if thou repeat them. Do not make enemies; the ruin of a man is in his tongue; guard thyself that thou make no loss." (36.) "Do not talk folly to all who come; the word of the day of the gossiping will turn thy house upside down." (31.) "Hold thyself far from rebels. He whose heart controls his mouth amongst the soldiers will certainly not be taken to the courts, nor be bound, nor know that which conciliates (presents)." (51.)

Covetousness is the fault particularly noted by Ptah-hotep, and he reminds one painfully of the failing of the present Egyptian. "If thou desirest thy going to be good, take thyself from all evil, beware of any covetous aim. That is as the painful disease of colic. He who entereth on it is not successful. It embroileth fathers and mothers with the mother's brothers, it separateth wife and husband. It is a thing that taketh to itself all evils, a bundle of all wickedness. A man liveth long whose rule is justice, who goeth according to its movements. He maketh a property thereby, while a covetous man hath no house." (19.)

Any remarks more on the need of not expecting to get the best of things. "Build thyself a house if thou dislike to live in common. Do not say 'This is a part of the house which has come to me by inheritance from my father and my mother who are in the tomb': for if thou comest to divide it with thy brother thy part will be the storerooms." (25.)

Commercial credit was much valued, more than we should expect in such a community. "Know thy tradesmen, for when thy affairs are unsuccessful thy good reputation with thy friends is a channel well filled, it is more important than a man's wealth. The property of one belongeth to another. A profitable thing is the good reputation of a man's son to him. The nature is better than the memory (acquirements)." (Ptahhotep, 35.)

The avoidance of drink and of luxury is dwelt on at length by Any, and was, doubtless, a needful warning in the XIXth Dynasty. "Do not be engrossed in the house where beer is drunk; for it is evil that words of another meaning come from thy mouth without thy being aware of having said them,—and that in falling thy limbs are broken without any person having laid hand on thee,—and that thy boon companions get up and say 'Turn out this drunkard,'—and when one comes to blame thee they find thee lying on the ground like a little child." (13.) And of the more refined pleasures he says, "There has been made for thee a feasting-place; the hedges have been put for thee around that which has been cultivated by the hoe for thee; there have been planted for thee in the inner parts sycomores, which join all the lands belonging to thy house; thou fillest thy hand with all flowers which thine eye sees. And one becomes weakened in the midst of all these, and happy is he who shall not abandon them." (Any, 23.)

52. Lastly, the uncertainty of life is strongly urged by Any. "Put this aim before thee, to reach a worthy old age, so that thou may be found to have completed thy house which is in the funereal valley, on the morning of burying thy body. Put this before thee in all the business which thine eye considers. When thou shalt be thus an old man, thou shalt lie down in the midst of them. There shall be no surprise to him who does well, he is prepared; thus when the messenger shall come to take thee,

he shall find one who is ready. Verily, thou shalt not have time to speak, for when he comes it shall be suddenly. Do not say, like a young man, 'Take thine ease, for thou shalt not know death.' When death cometh he will seize the infant who is in its mother's arms as he does him who has made an old age. Behold I have now told thee excellent things to be considered in thy heart, do them and thou shalt become a good man and all evils shall be far from thee." (Any, 15.)

Thus the main points of character in external matters were self-help, prudence, and respect for success; the value of knowledge, and of conciliation and fair speech for a hold on other men; avoiding the taint of covetousness, and keeping good credit; not being tied by mere pleasures, and being always ready to resign life. In all this the ancient Egyptian is much like the modern *fellah;* both accept their place in the world readily, and enjoy it quietly without being overweighted by duty. Neither of these know anything of the Western sense of the terrible responsibilities of life, and the tyranny of the conscience. They simply enjoy living without being too particular, and lay great stress on making it as pleasant as possible to other people. Their aim was to be easy, good-natured, quiet gentlemen, who made life as agreeable as they could all round. And though the ideal was not a very high one, it was not bad for a warm climate; and it may compare well with the actual practice of our own land or any other.

FAMILY DUTIES

53. The position of women was always an important one in Egypt, as the social system was matriarchal in the early times, and continued to place property in the hands of women throughout the history. Even the strongly patriarchal Roman law and the power of Islam did not root out this, as in Makrisi's time a Copt always said, in selling anything, "with my wife's permission"; and to the present time in Upper Egypt women are the treasurers and misers of the household. Yet the relation was apparently much on the same footing as other business, and has little of the family character; nor did it produce any large number of precepts.

Throughout all the earlier history a woman who had property was always mistress of the house, and her husband was a sort of boarder or visitor, who had to keep up the establishment. This is seen even in the XIXth Dynasty, where Any writes, "Be not rude to a woman in her house if thou know her thoroughly. Do not say, 'Where is that? bring it to me,' when she hath put it in its right place, and thine eye hath seen it; when thou art silent thou knowest her qualities, and it is a joy for thine hand to be with her. There are many who understand not how a man should act if he wish to bring misfortune into her house, and who know not how to find out her conduct in all ways. The man who is strong of heart is soon master in her house." (Any, 56.) And even in the Ptolemaic times marriage contracts made over all possible property of the man entirely to the woman.

In most nations, however, there have been several legal forms of marriage side by side; in ancient India and in Roman law this was conspicuous. Probably the same diversity existed in Egypt, depending on the question of whether the woman had property of her own to begin with. In Ptah-hotep we find: "If thou art successful and hast furnished thy house and lovest the wife of thy bosom, then fill her stomach and clothe her back. The medicine for her body is oil. Make glad her heart during the time that thou hast. She is a field profitable to its owner." (21.) In later times the Ptolemaic precepts say, "May it not happen to thee to maltreat thy wife, whose strength is less than thine; but may she find in thee a protector." (Precepts, 8.) Here the husband is presumed to be independent, and to be master.

Irregularities are considered by Ptah-hotep to demand at least compensatory kindness. " If thou makest a woman ashamed, wanton of heart, whom her fellow townspeople know to be under two laws (in an ambiguous position); be kind to her for a season, send her not away, let her have food to eat. The wantonness of her heart appreciateth a straight path." (Ptah-hotep, 37.) But he warns most strongly against a corrupt life. "If thou wishest to prolong friendship in a house into which thou enterest as master, as brother, as friend, in any place that thou enterest beware of approaching to women; no place in which that is done prospereth. The face is not watchful in attaining it (pleasures); a thousand men are injured in order to be profited for a little moment, like a dream, by tasting which death is reached." (Ptah-hotep, 18.) Any similarly says, "Follow not after a woman, and allow not that she occupy thy heart." (Any, 57.) And of the wandering professional he says, "Keep thyself from the strange woman, who is not known in her town. Look not on her when she cometh, and know her not, and fill not thy heart with her. She is a whirlpool in deep water, the vortex of which is not known. The woman whose husband is afar writeth to thee daily; when none is there to see her she standeth and spreadeth her snare; sin unto death it is to hearken thereto, even when she shall not have accomplished her plan in reality. Men do all crimes for this alone." (Any, 8.)

In the qualifications for the kingdom of Osiris the moral law was early laid down. In the earlier repudiation it appears to be only a trespass against the sacred property, "I have not committed fornication nor impurity, in what was sacred to the god of my city." (A. 22.) But in the later repudiation this is divided into three general propositions. "I have not committed adultery with another man's wife" (B. 19); "I have not been impure"

(B. 20); "I have not been given to unnatural lust." (B. 27.)

54. Of the parental and filial duties there is not much said, compared with the space they fill in the systems of the further east. There is not a single condition laid down on these duties in the judgment before Osiris; and according to these earliest codes a man had no stronger duties to his parents than to any other persons. The early moralists, however, treat of such duties to some extent, but they again almost disappear in the later writers. As compared with the code of harsher climates this may be due to the small amount of cost and care of children; and as compared with other eastern lands, the provision of offerings in semblance by the Egyptians in the tomb left little place for the urgency of filial duties in maintaining continual supplies for the deceased. It is at least a curious lack, contrary to what might be expected in the Egyptian code. We read in Kagemni of the "man devoid of sociability," that he is "rude to his mother and to his people" (Kagemni, 4); and the late Precepts echo this, "Make it not in the heart of a mother to enter into bitter-

ness." (1.) And in Any we specially read of the long cares of a mother, and the consequent duty to do the same for the next generation. (Any, 40.) He enjoins the duty of funeral offerings: "Offer water to thy father and thy mother who rest in the valley (of tombs); see to the water, and offer the divine things which are said to be acceptable. Forget it not when thou art far off; if thou dost this thy son shall also do the same for thee." (Any, 12.)

The value of paternal precepts is also dwelt on. "If the son of a man receive what his father saith, no plan of his shall fail. He whom thou teachest as thy son, or the listener that is successful in the heart of the nobles, he guideth his mouth according to what he hath been told . . . . He faileth that entereth without hearing. He that knoweth, on the next day is established; he who is ignorant is crushed." (Ptah-hotep, 39.) "The son that hearkeneth is a follower of Horus; there is good for him when he hath hearkened; he groweth old, he reacheth *amakh*, he telleth the like to his children, renewing the teaching of his father. Every man teacheth as he hath performed; he telleth the like to his sons that they may tell it again to their children." (Ptah-hotep, 41.) "Do according to that which thy master telleth thee. How excellent to a man is the teaching of his father, out of whom he hath come, out of his very body, and who spoke unto him while he was yet altogether in his loins. Greater is what hath been done unto him, than what hath been said unto him. Behold a good son that god giveth doeth beyond what he is told for his master; he doeth right, doing heartily, even as thou hast come unto me . . . ." (Ptah-hotep, 43.) The inheritance of qualities, and their importance above education, is here well marked.

The duties to the children are also enforced. Any says, "Take to thyself a wife when young, that she may give thee a son; being thine, a child to thee, when thou art a young man, is a witness that this is a good man's deed, of one whom many will praise the more for his son." (1.) And Ptah-hotep says, "If thou art a successful man, and thou makest a son by god's grace, if he is accurate, goeth again in thy way, and attendeth to thy business on the proper occasion, do unto him every good thing, for he is thy own son, to whom it belongeth that thy *ka* begat; estrange not thy heart from him." (Ptah-hotep, 12.) And in the late precepts the duties and care for sons are also repeated, though the strong notion of continuity of family occupation and tradition seems to have gone. "May it not happen to thee to cause thy infant to suffer if he be weak, but assist him." (Precepts, 14.) "Do not abandon one son to another of thy sons, who is stronger or more courageous." (Precepts, 15.) And this control extended into maturity, for we read, "Do not allow thy son to be familiar with a married woman." (Precepts, 18.)

LECTURE VII.

THE OUTER DUTIES

RELATIONS TO EQUALS

55. THE more general duties to equals occupy a large part of the repudiation of sins. The earlier list says, "I have not murdered" (A. 16), and "I have not commanded murder" (A. 17); and the second list states, "I have not slain men." (B. 5.) In the late precepts there appears the higher command, "Do not save thy life at the cost of that of another." (Precepts, 12.)

The general statement with which the earlier repudiation opens, "I have not done injury to men" (A. 1), is amplified into several different declarations in the later list. "I have not done injustice" (B. 1) opens the second list, and further it declares, "I have not robbed" (B. 2), "I have not stolen" (B. 14 and 15), "I have not been a pilferer." (B. 16.) Special forms of dishonesty are detailed: "I have not added to nor diminished the measures of grain (A. 23), and in the second list, "I have not diminished the corn measure" (B. 6), "I have not diminished the palm measure" (A. 24), "I have not falsified the cubit of land" (A. 25), "I have not added to the weight of the balance" (A. 26), "I have not nullified the plummet of the scales." (A. 26*a*.) The sins of Egyptian agriculture are named: "I have not stopped water in its season" (A. 31), "I have not dammed running water." (A 32.)

A very strange repudiation next appears which seems as if fire was looked on as having a separate being. "I have not quenched fire in its moment," *i.e.* when burning up. (A. 33.) Possibly fire was looked on as a portion of the sun-god, who would be offended at being thwarted.

The earlier repudiation does not name falsehood, but the later says, "I have not spoken falsehood" (B. 9), and "I have not deceived nor done ill." (B. 34.)

56. Consideration for others is strongly put forward. "Look not a second time on what thine eye has seen in thine house; and being silent do not let it be openly spoken of by another." (Any, 7.) In the second

repudiation of sins we find, "I have not made (unjust) preferences" (B. 40), "I have not played the rich man, except in my own things" (B. 41), "I am not of an aggressive hand." (B. 30.) Antef claims, "I am one that smooths difficulties, respecting (?) a name, divining (?) what is in the heart" (3). "I am one prudent in preventing and easing, quieting the mourner with pleasant speech" (4).

Liberality was enjoined, as in the Song of the Harper to Neferhotep, "Give bread to him who is without a plot of land"; and the second repudiation has, "I have not been niggardly in grain." (B. 14.) While Ptah-hotep requires that liberality should be genial—"Let thy face be shining the time that thou hast for a feast; verily that which cometh out of the store-chamber doth not go back again, but is bread for apportionment; and he that is niggardly is an accuser, empty is his belly." (Ptah-hotep, 34.)

The general duties of goodwill and kindness to men are often repeated. In the earlier repudiation we find, "I have not caused suffering to men" (A. 18), "I have not done mischief" (A. 5); while in the later list this is repeated as "I have not caused weeping" (B. 26), "I have not made a disturbance" (B. 21), "I have not borne a grudge" (B. 28). Violent and harsh conduct is specially condemned by the moralists, "Make not terror amongst men, god punisheth the like . . . never did violence prosper." (Ptah-hotep, 6.) And "If thy conciliatory speech is good, they shall incline the heart to take it." (Any, 61.) "I am good, not hasty of countenance, not pulling a man headlong," (?) says Antef. (16.) "Let no punishment be done when a noble is busy; do not depress the heart of him that is already laden." (Ptah-hotep, 26.) This last maxim gives a good view of the Egyptian attitude of mind towards punishments; they were no vindictive pleasure to the Egyptians, on the contrary they gave a sympathetic pain to them, and the sight was so unpleasant and depressing that it should be postponed rather than annoy a high official who was already worried with business. It may be doubted if any ancient people have had such an aversion to causing pain or distress as is shown by the genial and kindly upper classes of the Vth Dynasty. It is the very antithesis of the Greek slaughter of prisoners, the Roman games, or the patristic hell.

The precepts of friendship are what might be expected in such a society: kindly and prudent, but without any passionate depth of feeling. "It befalleth that a quarrelsome man is a spoiler of things: be not thus to him who cometh to thee; the remembrance of a man is of his kindliness in the years after the staff." (Ptah-hotep, 34.) "Useful are the doings of a friend (if he) purify himself from evils, (then) thou shalt be safe from his being lost; (therefore) beware of any loss (of friendship)." (Any, 52.) And in the late precepts of a base society it was enjoined, "Do not pervert the heart of thy acquaintance if he be pure." (Precept, 23.) While caution in friendship was noted very early. "If thou seekest the character of a friend, mind thou do not ask (of others); go to him, occupy thyself with him alone, so as not to interfere with his business; argue with him after a season, test his heart with an instance of speech." (Ptah-hotep, 33.)

57. The position of a leading man is dwelt on by Ptah-hotep. "If thou art strong, inspiring awe by knowledge or by pleasing, speak in first command; that is to say, not according to (another's) lead. The weak man entereth into error. Raise not thine heart

lest it should be cast down. Be not silent. Beware of interruption and of answering words with heat. The flames of a fiery heart sweep away the mild man when a fighter treadeth on his path." (Ptah-hotep, 25.) Antef says, "I am a speaker in the house of justice, of ready mouth in the difficulties of heart." (20.) "If thou art a guide, commanding the conduct of a company, seek for thyself every good aim, so that thy policy may be without error. A great thing is justice, enduring and surviving." (Ptah-hotep, 5.) "I am accurate like the balance, weighing truth like Thoth," says Antef. (17.) "Do not take a haughty attitude," is said in the Ptolemaic precepts. (24.)

The business of the council of the district was an important part of the life of a wellborn Egyptian; it was the main field for the use of most of the social qualities, much what the modern *meglis* is among the shekhs of an Egyptian town, or the bench of Justices of the Peace in England. We have already noticed allusions to qualities at the council, and some injunctions relate entirely to such affairs. "If thou art a successful man sitting in the council of his lord, confine thine heart to what promiseth success. That thou shouldest be silent is better than that thy speech should run wild. Thou knowest what thou understandest. It is an expert that speaketh in the council. Ill to bear is speaking of every kind of work. It is one that understandeth it that putteth it to the stick." (Ptah-hotep, 24.) "If thou actest as the son of a man upon the council, a messenger to persuade the people. . . . do not tend to favour one side. Beware lest it be said 'His method is that of the nobles, he giveth speech favouring one side therein.' Turn thine aim unto an even balance." (Ptah-hotep, 28.) "If thou findest a debater in his moment, a poor man, not thine equal, let not thine heart leap out upon him when he is feeble. Let him alone, let him refute himself, question him not over-much." (Ptah-hotep, 4): a saying that reminds us of George Herbert's :

> "Fierceness makes
> Error a fault, and truth discourtesy."

Lastly, convivial conduct has its duties laid down by one of the earliest moralists, Kagemni. "If thou sittest at meat with a company, hate the bread that thou desirest, for it is but a little moment. Restrain appetite, for gluttony is base. It is a base fellow who is mastered by his belly, who passeth time without thought, free ranging for his feeding in their houses. But be not afraid of meat in company with the greedy, take what he giveth thee, refuse it not, thinking that it will honour him. If there be a man devoid of making himself known, on whom no word hath power . . . . every one crieth, ' Let thy name come forth, thou art silent with the mouth when spoken to.' " (Kagemni, 2, 3, 4.)

RELATIONS TO SUPERIORS

58. Strange to say not a single duty to superiors appears in the great repudiation of sins. The total absence of family duties and those to superiors in these primitive categories may possibly lead us to the view that neither family nor superiors existed in the early period of society to which these lists belong. It would be quite possible that in the matriarchal society the permanent bond of the family was not looked on as entailing duties different in kind to those equally due

THE OUTER DUTIES 147

to relatives and neighbours in general. And it would be also possible that in a population of independent farmers without any central organization, or need of combining against foes, the upper class for whom such formularies were prepared had practically no superiors to whom they owed duties. Very likely the eldest or most able farmer of a district would be a sort of leader; but practically a council of the landowners of the neighbourhood might be the only authority, and no obligations to any superiors of these would exist. Certainly in the historical ages of the Vth and XIXth Dynasties the family duties are far more lightly touched on than we should expect, and there is none of that clannish sense of solidarity which is the basis of society to western peoples; while the duties to superiors are not so frequently named as the duties to inferiors. The absence of certain classes of feeling and ideas may often show us more than the presence of particular injunctions.

The duty of respect to old age is of course one of the most obvious to many different races. Yet we do not find this enjoined in the earlier sayings, but only in

Ptolemaic times. "Mock not the venerable man who is thy superior." (Precept 25.) "May it happen to thee to respect the venerable." (Precept 7.) And the master is equally to be regarded. "Curse not thy master before god." (Precept 9.) "Do not speak against thy master." (Precept 10.) And, earlier than that, age was to be respected more than position. "Do not thou sit when another is standing who is older than thee, even if thou art greater than he in his office." (Any, 27.)

Maxims for servants are also given by Any. "He who hates laziness comes without being called." (46.) "When none call him the runner comes." (47.) "Reply not to a superior who is annoyed, wait on one side; speak softly when he speaks in anger, this remedy appeases his heart." (58.)

The relations of subordinates to nobles occupy much notice. The semi-domestic staff of business agents attached to the household of the wealthy chief of a district, is well known even under the civilized government of the present day; but when the bonds of order in Egypt were far slacker than now, when each petty chief, or big shekh, was responsible for the peace of his district and for its taxes to the king, with unlimited powers for keeping order in his hands, these staffs of servants really included the police, taxgatherers, accountants, and district surveyors of the petty jurisdiction of their lord. Hence they were a numerous and important class, in fact the bureaucracy of the country. Ptah-hotep enjoins, "If thou art a man of those who sit at the place of a greater man than thyself take what he giveth .... thou shalt look at what is before thee: pierce him not with many glances, it is abomination to the *ka* for them to be directed at him. Speak not unto him until he calleth, one knoweth not the evil (or sorrow) at heart; thou shalt speak when he questioneth thee, and so what thou sayest will be good to the heart." (7.) "The noble who hath plenty of bread doeth as his *ka* commandeth, he will give to whom he praiseth, it is the manner of evening (the common supper of the whole household). It befalleth that it is the *ka* that openeth his hands. The noble giveth, it is not the subject who winneth. The eating of bread is under the disposal of god, it is the ignorant that rebelleth against it." (7.) This picture of conduct in the noble's household is exactly what may be seen every evening at the round supper of a wealthy man. Antef says, " I am a regulator for the king's house, knowing what is said in every *diwan*." (12.) " I am a pleasure unto the house of his master, bringing to remembrance his successful exploits." (14.)

59. In business we read, " Bend thy back to thy chief, the superior of the king's house on whose property thy house dependeth, and thy payments in their proper place. It is ill to be at variance with the chief, one liveth only while he is gracious. . . ." (Ptah-hotep, 31.) " Teach a noble what is profitable to him; make him acceptable amongst people, let his satisfaction reach his master on whose *ka* depend thy provisions. When the stomach of a favourite is satisfied, thy back will be clothed thereby." (Ptah-hotep, 27.) Here back-stairs influence and the evils of toadying are plainly commended. Antef boasts, " I am one exact in the house of his master, knowing the return in trade." (?) (7.) " I am one that recognizes his instructor, that recognizes a counsellor; a councillor that causes his counsel to be taken." (19.)

To negotiators and envoys some very

judicious orders are given. "If thou art a man that entereth, sent by a noble to a noble, be exact in the manner of him who sendeth thee, do the business for him as he saith. Beware of making ill feeling by words that would set noble against noble, in destroying justice (or good order); do not exaggerate. The washing of the heart shall not be repeated in the speech of any man, noble or commoner; that is an abomination to the *ka*." (8.) This "washing of the heart" is evidently the free unguarded expression of feeling about a person, known to us as "letting fly," "expressing the feelings," "using language," &c., a process well known to wash the heart by clearing away ill feeling, after which the speaker "feels better." To repeat any of this was a high breach of good faith; only the exact message which was sent should be repeated. "I am firm of foot, excellent of plan, forcing the way for him that establisheth him," is the business-like boast of Antef's capacity as envoy. (18.) Those who sought justice were reminded that they must not be touchy if they could not be attended to at once. "When thou art in the council-hall, standing and sitting until thy going (or the movement of thy business) that hath been commanded for thee on the earliest day, go not away if thou art kept back, while the face (of the chief) is attentive to him who entereth and reporteth, and the place of him who is called is broad. The council-hall is according to rule, and all its method according to measure. It is god who promoteth position, it is not done for those who are ready of elbows." (Ptah-hotep, 13).

And even in death presumption was not to be tolerated: "Do not build up thy tomb above those who command thee." (Precepts, 5.)

RELATIONS TO INFERIORS

60. On the duties and relations to inferiors the repudiations of sins have much to say. The claim that "I have not oppressed those beneath me" (A. 2) is echoed down to the Ptolemaic times, "May it not happen to thee to maltreat an inferior" (Precept 7), and "Do not amuse thyself by playing upon those who are dependent upon thee." (Precept 17.)

The repudiation continues, "I have not caused a slave to be ill-treated by his overseer" (A. 13); "I have not caused weeping" (A. 16); "I am one silent to the violent and ignorant, from a desire to abolish greediness of oppression." (Antef, 1.)

With the fine sense of reserve that we have noticed before, even a favour to a subordinate was not to be recalled to notice if he were ungrateful enough to forget it. "If thou art gracious concerning a matter that hath happened, and leanest to favour a man in his right, avoid the subject, and do not recall it after the first day that he hath been silent to thee (about it)." (Ptah-hotep, 29.)

Of the management of inferiors we read, "The leader of a party going to the field seems another being." (Any, 53.) "Let there be a life of discipline in thy house; reprimand is healthy for thy finding out for thyself." (Any, 20.) But the care and attention was not to be confined to the house. "My god having granted that thou hast children, the heart of thy father knows them (they are cared for); but whoever is hungry is satisfied in his own house, and I am the wall which protects him. Do nothing without thy heart (cordiality), for it is my god who gives existence." (Any, 26.) And long before in the repudiations of sins the soul declared, "I have not caused hunger" (A. 15), "I have not brought any to hunger" (A. 14), "I have not taken food away" (B. 10), "I have not taken milk from the mouth of babes" (A. 27), referring to his not having harried the women of the estate with farm work. And overworking the serfs was specially forbidden: "I have not made a man do more than his day's work" is in the earlier repudiation. (A. 6.)

The avoidance of pride after prosperity is enjoined: "Eat not bread while another stands, without reaching out thy hand for him. It is known eternally that the man who is not, will become one rich, another poor, but food will (always) remain for him who acts charitably. A man may be rich for years and yet become a servant next year." (Any, 41.) "If thou growest great after small things, and makest wealth after poverty, so that thou art an example thereof in thy city, thou art known in thy nome, and thou art become prominent; then do not wrap up thy heart in thy riches that have come to thee by the gift of god (for there shall follow) another like unto thee to whom the like hath befallen." (Ptah-hotep, 30.)

61. Grasping ways were specially in-

veighed against: "I am one open of face to his mendicant, doing good to his equal." (5.) "I am open of face, of bountiful hand, master of hospitality, free of hiding the face" (8), "I am the friend of the miserable, sweet and pleasant to him who hath nothing" (9), "I am food for the hungry who hath nothing, and of bountiful hand to the miserable" (10) are the boasts of Antef. "Let not thy heart be extortionate about shares, in grasping at what is not thy portion. Let not thy heart be extortionate towards thy neighbours. Greater is prayer to a kindly person than force. Poor is he that carrieth off his neighbours without the persuasion of words. A little for which there hath been extortion causeth remorse when the stomach is cool." (Ptah-hotep, 20.)

The fair treatment and encouragement of those who seek justice is commanded. "If thou art an adviser be pleased to hear the speech of a petitioner, let him not hesitate to empty himself of what he hath purposed to tell thee; love beareth away falsification (or concealment), let his heart be washed until that is accomplished for which he hath come. If a hesitating man make complaints one (a bystander) saith,

'Why when a man hath trespassed are there no complaints made to him (the judge) about what hath happened?' It is good breeding to hear graciously." (Ptah-hotep, 17.) Antef says, "I am a judge hearing truth, advising (?) what is in the happy mean" (13), "I am pleasant in the *diwans*, attentive, without piggishness." (15.)

The steward or farm bailiff was always a very important person, as he could make or mar any man, and might readily play false. "Take a steward of just repute, for thy reputation is in his balance ... spare thy hand from him who is in thy dwellings, the other things being in his care." (Any, 17.) This free dealing with a trusty steward is commanded. "Degrade not the steward, who acts as deputy in thy house. Let him not run after thy ear. Give him audience when he is in thy house, and turn not back his requests. Speak to him honourably, being honourable on earth without reproach for what he does." (Any, 63.) But due caution was needed before trusting a man thus. "Do not open thy hand to an unknown man, it will be a loss to thee. When goods are put in their store-rooms he becomes to thee as a deputy, and will store thy things for himself, and thy people will find him in the way to thee." (Any, 18.) The last touch is particularly true in Egypt, where any man who is in a place of trust is soon in the position of a go-between, preventing his master from seeing too much of those below him.

Of assistance to others Antef boasts thus: "I am knowledge to him that knoweth not, teaching a man what is advantageous to him." (11.)

Coming down to animals we find a curious code of fair play enjoined in the first repudiation of sins. Animals might be caught in open ways, but not by deceit. "I have not caught animals by a bait of herbage; I have not trapped birds by a bait of "gods' bones"; I have not caught fish by a bait of fishes' bodies." (A. 28, 29, 30.)

DUTIES TO THE GODS

62. The duties enjoined toward the gods are of interest as showing somewhat of the lay Egyptian's attitude toward religion, and giving somewhat of a different side to that of the temple scenes. It is to be noticed that there is not a single maxim on this

subject in those of Kagemni and Ptahhotep. Regarding the king — the great high priest — the soul declared, "I have not cursed the king." (B. 35.)

In the duties about the tomb, the earlier repudiation has, "I have not taken the provisions of the blessed dead." (A. 21.) And in late times when ostentation abounded the precepts enjoined, "Build not thy tomb in thine own estate; build not thy tomb at the approaches to the temples." (19, 20.)

The offerings to the gods were specially guarded in the earlier repudiation, "I have not cut short the rations of the temples" (A. 19), "I have not diminished the offerings of the gods" (A. 20), "I have not defrauded the cycle of the gods of their choice meats." (A. 34.) The sacred property was also guarded, "I have not stolen the property of the gods" (B. 8), "I have not driven off the cattle of the sacred lands" (A. 35), "I have not slain a sacred animal." (B. 13.)

A strange injunction is, "I have not stopped a god in his comings forth." (A. 36.) This almost looks as if it referred to checking idiots or insane persons, who are generally supposed to be possessed.

Offence to the gods was also guarded against; "I have not done that which is an abomination to the gods" (A. 12), "I have not offended the gods of any city" (B. 42), "I have not cursed god." (B. 38.)

63. Some form of augury seems to be referred to by Any in the remark, "If one comes to seek thy views, it is a reason to consult the sacred books." (Any 3.) The duty of making offerings is often repeated. In the earlier repudiation it occurs, "I approach the bark of offerings, I approach the place of him who offers the prescribed offerings." (A. 7.) Any says, "Make the feast of thy god, renew it in its season, it irritates god to neglect it; set up witnesses after thou hast made thy offering the first time of so doing." (Any, 2.) Again, "When thou makest an offering to thy god, guard against his abominations . . . . Do not increase his orders; guard thyself from expanding his liturgies; thine eye should regard his plans. Apply thyself to make adoration in his name, for it is he who gives to spirits millions of forms, magnifying those who magnify him. The god of this earth being Shu, lord of the horizon, and his emblems being on earth, as one gives him

incense with bread every day, he will make to flourish by his appearing that which is planted. Increase therefore the bread for the god." (Any, 39.) "Give thyself to the god; guard thyself each day for the god, and do to-morrow as to-day. Sacrifice, for god looks on the offerer, but he neglects those who neglect him." (Any, 48.) "He who exalts his spirit by praise, by adoration, by incense in his works, so that devotion is in his affairs—he who does thus god shall magnify his name." (Any, 5.) A somewhat higher line is touched by Any in one case, "That which is detestable in the sanctuary of god are noisy feasts; if thou implore him with a loving heart of which all the words are mysterious, he will do thy matters, he hears thy words, he accepts thine offerings." (Any, 11.)

64. We have already noticed in dealing with the inner character, how strength, quietness, and the avoiding of extremes was set forth as the aim in cultivating the mind; and how, in external business, self-help, prudence, conciliation, and honesty are enjoined. We may now sum up the principles of dealing with others. The family duties we have seen are very little dwelt on; and there

seems no sense of the wider range of duties to relatives that carries so much with it to our notions. In dealing with equals, beside the obvious crimes of murder and theft, cheating and falsehood are strongly repudiated; faults should be overlooked; oppression and stinginess should be avoided; and no mere mischief or needless suffering should be allowed, because it was unpleasant to see as well as to feel. Friendship was looked on as useful, but without any enthusiasm or devotion. Haughtiness was to be eschewed, and geniality cultivated in social intercourse. To superiors, ready submission was commended; and the influences of back-stairs and toadying were not to be omitted. But mischief should not be made by repeating strong expressions. To inferiors, fairness and kindness was enjoined; past favour should not be harped upon. Pride, grasping, and brow-beating are all condemned. Trusty servants should be respected, and not humiliated, and animals should be hunted fairly and without deception. But with the gods everything was a matter of *quid pro quo*, and making terms in the style of Jacob.

Now the whole of this is rather the spirit of the eighteenth than of the nineteenth century. Their virtues are quiet and discreet; their vices are calculating. They belong far more to the tone of Chesterfield or Gibbon than to that of Kingsley or Carlyle; they accord with Pope or Thomson rather than with Swinburne or Tennyson. There is hardly a single splendid feeling; there is not one burst of magnanimous sacrifice; there is not one heartfelt self-depreciation, in any point of all this worldly-wisdom. They are as canny as a Scot, without his sentiment; as prudent as a Frenchman, without his ideals; as self-conceited as an Englishman, without his family.

On the other hand we must recognize that the Egyptians show a wealth of good qualities—good, but not lovable—of sterling value for the constitution of society, which gave them the high place which they filled in the early history of man.

But all this is the standard and not the practice. The standard is not so very high that we should assume that the practice was much lower; it was a practicable standard, and was probably effective in laying hold of a large part of the people. Cold and hard as much of it seems, we yet know from their stories and their songs that they had much fuller feelings than would be expected from the maxims of the prudent. And we must no more judge them entirely by the cautious injunctions of their ancients, than we should wish our own selves to be pictured in the future as being all Benthams and Mills, Pecksniffs or Pitt-Crawleys.

NOTES

A. INHERITED INTUITIONS.
B. THE IDEAL OF TRUTH, LUCIAN.
C. STATISTICS OF CONSCIENCE MONEY.
D. NATURE OF THE *KA*.

NOTE A.

INHERITED INTUITIONS

As an analogy to the view of inherited intuitions of moral sense and conscience selecting lines of action, there is a similar inheritance in the sense of pain and pleasure. The extraordinary theories of special nerves of pain, and the difficulties of defining it from pleasure, are all needless when we recognize the inherited character of such definitions. Simple sensation is the common basis of both; and such sensations as ancestral and personal experience have associated on the average with injury are recognized as pain, those associated with well-being are recognized as pleasure. The ideas of pain or pleasure are entirely an association of causes and effects, and nothing abstractly different in nature. The pains which cannot be inherited, as those of decay and death, are not in the least a dread to animals, nor to races of men, who are not reflective—pointing clearly to the inherited and acquired idea of pain. During recovery there may be far sharper and more lasting sensations than during injury, and yet they are always pleasurable, showing that not the intensity but the connection of the sensation gives its character. This again is seen by the intense misery of internal injury, without any keen sensations; association here is the cause of pain. Even a short experience of the individual will decide between pain or pleasure of a sensation; a medicine, such as quinine, which may be very nauseous at first, will become a pleasure like a sweetmeat when it has been associated with relief. And new flavours unlike any yet known, as new fruits or chemical compounds, cannot be distinguished as nice or nasty at first. It is only when their effects have been felt that a sense of pain or pleasure becomes associated with them; thus showing that association alone produces the character of a sensation.

If, thus, pains and pleasures are purely associative ideas, inherited, and developed in the individual, the mental ideas of right and wrong are all the more likely to be an inheritance of trains of thought and ideas which have proved to be successful or injurious.

NOTE B.

THE IDEAL OF TRUTH

As a good study of the sense of veracity in the later Greek world, we may note a piece of one of Lucian's Dialogues ("The Liar," No. 52).

"TYCHIADES. Can you tell me, Philocles, what is the attraction which makes most men love to tell lies? They even go to the point of saying things which have not common sense, and listen to those who do likewise.

"PHILOCLES. There are plenty of reasons, Tychiades, enough to make such men lie as only think of their self-interest.

"TYCHIADES. But the question is not there, as one says, for I am not speaking of those who lie to be useful to themselves. Some such are praiseworthy when they have deceived enemies, or when in a critical moment they have employed this remedy as a means of safety; it is thus that Ulysses often acted to guide his life and those of his companions. But I am speaking, my dear, of those folks who without any need much prefer lies to truth, and please themselves and make a business of it without any particular reason.

"PHILOCLES. And have you known folks of this kind, who have an innate love of lying?

"TYCHIADES. Certainly, plenty of them."

NOTE C.

CONSCIENCE MONEY

SOME further details about Conscience Money that do not concern the immediate argument of the lecture may be given here, as this subject is one that has not yet been studied. I am indebted to the kindness of Mr. Robert Chalmers, of H.M. Treasury, for informing me what materials were available on this matter, and for obtaining the permission of the Chancellor of the Exchequer to enable me to have the details of amounts copied for my use by a clerk. These copies only concern the dates and amounts received, as the information about source or persons involved is, of course, essentially private to the Department. The entries of the last thirty years comprise 4791 items received, ranging from 1d. to £4070. All of these have been tabulated and worked up in the present enquiry.

The first question is how the material should be dealt with so as to obtain the most intelligible result. The long lists of varying sums have to be classified and arranged. The first question is that of the scale. In the appendix to the *Pyramids and Temples of Gizeh* I pointed out how a scale of equal increments was not the true basis of the equilateral probability curve. The difference between this and a scale of equal multiples is not seen except where the variation is a large part of the total amount. Hence in most physical questions it is never thought of. But when dealing with variations of many times the total quantity—as here a variation of one to a million in the amount—then the scale is an essential question. When we look at any physical variable of which the reciprocal is likely to be treated, as for instance the distance or angular parallax of stars, the density or volume of a given mass, the fractions of an atmosphere of pressure, or the pressure in height of mercury—in each case it would be clearly wrong to get different curves from the results because we read them on a different method. Such difference of curves would simply prove an irrationality of the scales. But no such difference of results can exist if we use a scale of equal multiples, or a logarithmic scale. Such was the reasoning then used.

Now Conscience Money is an excellent subject by which to test the validity of this reasoning. It varies so enormously that any scale not true in theory could never yield a consistent probability curve from such material. But we see on plotting out the amounts on the scale of equal multiples that we reach a consistent equilateral curve with no more divergence than can easily be explained. Any scale that was not true in theory could never deal so equably with material varying so vastly in amount as from 1d. to £4,000. This result is, then, one of the effective proofs of the *a priori* reasoning given above, that the true scale is one of equal multiples, and that probable error is really × or ÷ x and not + or − x.

Next comes the question of what divisions are most rational for dealing with the material. The £5 note is one of the main features, and it would be obviously wrong to divide the scale so that such a main factor would come just at either limit of a division. It should be central. And as £2 10s. and £10 are the next most obvious amounts we are led to a scale of binary multiples, where £2 10s., £5, £10, £20, will each be the centre of a group. Hence the dividing points fall at $\sqrt{2}$ × these amounts, or £3 10s. 8d., £7 1s. 5d.; and halving and doubling these limits, down to 1½d. and up to £3620 5s. 4d.

Such was the settlement of the nature of the scale and of its rational divisions for dealing with this particular material.

Beside the main total curve of the number of payments made, the amounts of which lie between the successive divisions of such a scale, there are also curves given of lesser portions of the whole material.

The "curve of 1887-97" is of value to show the real meaning of the sudden start up in the middle of the total curve. This I referred to the facility of sending a £5 note anonymously and through the post. This facility induced men to postpone sending what conscience demanded when over £1 until it amounted to £5 ; thus making the curve of payments first fall below the probability curve and then start above it at £5. Similarly the £5 facility forestalled the action of conscience and made men send in payments which would otherwise have been left to accumulate ; thus it actually diminished the frequency of larger amounts. Now this erratic variation has disappeared in the returns of the last ten years, and there is hardly any of it to be seen in the "curve of 1887-97." The reason of this change seems to be very probably the introduction of postal orders, by which anonymous payments of sums under £5 can be as easily made as by the old £5 note.

Then another enquiry is as to the different types of conscience. The commonest type is but vague, and sends lump sums without much caring if they exactly make up for deficiencies. The Conscience Money becomes a sort of free-will offering to atone for past deficiencies and keep an easy mind on the subject. A small number of people are more exact, however, and it is these higher classes of conscience that are shown by the curves of "amounts exact to $\frac{1}{5}$," that is to say any even number of pounds or of shillings, such as 6, 7, 8, 9, 11, 12, 13, 14, 16, 17, etc. ; "amounts exact to $\frac{1}{50}$," or precise to the nearest shilling on £2 10s. or more ; and "amounts exact to $\frac{1}{500}$," or the nearest penny on £2 or shilling on £25. It will be seen that the centres of these curves are successively lower and lower along the scale, showing that the more precise types of conscience belong to those persons who deal with smaller amounts.

Another interesting question is the seasonal distribution.

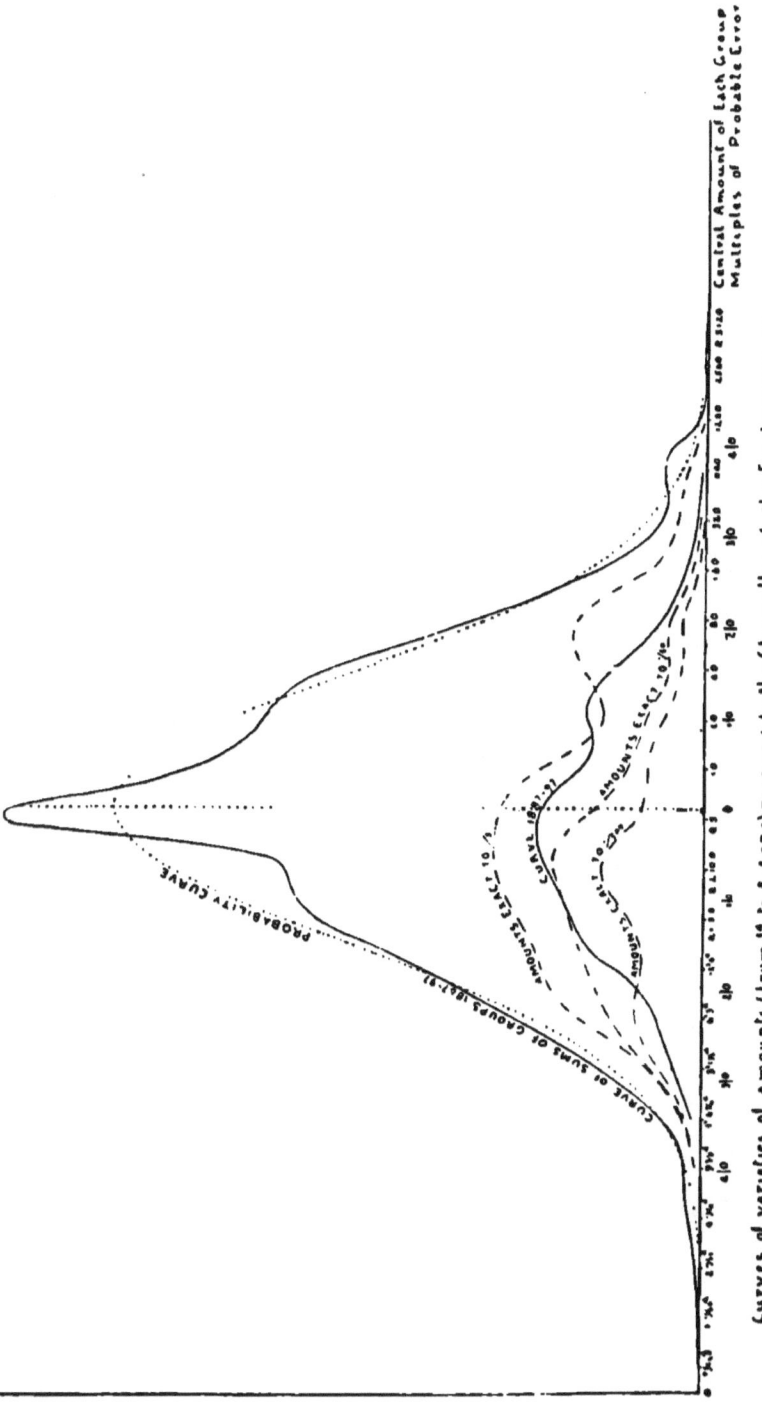

The effect of Christmas or quarterly settlements is not traceable at all. But a well-marked variation exists, amounting to double (both in the curve of frequency, and in the curve of the total amount) at one time of the year, to what it is at another. The *maximum* is in March, the *minimum* is in September. The meaning of this appears to be that spare cash is most abundant in March and least in September. And the cause probably is that as savings accumulate during the more economical season of the winter months, conscience can have freer sway. When warm weather and excursions begin to be in view money is kept back for them, and the end of the summer holidays is the time when conscience has least chance, and has to put up with promises of the future.

From all this we can see a little of the practical working and nature of conscience in a certain class. It easily puts up with postponement; but has a permanent hold, and exacts its claims when the most convenient opportunity occurs; whether that opportunity be the easy sending of a £5 note, or the paying up when money has fewest claims upon it. It is more precise and exacting among those persons who deal with rather smaller amounts than with others. And it is as legitimately and honestly followed in great things, great temptations and opportunities, as it is in small matters. Such results, though rather vague, are of unique interest in this part of ethics and psychology, as somewhat confirming and somewhat enlarging our *a priori* notions of what would be likely, and giving a definite and real basis of observation.

To gain some comparative light upon the matter I enquired of two friends abroad what were the views in their countries. A French Professor replies: "What you call 'Conscience Money' exists amongst us, but I do not remember having seen any published details of such restitutions; the State accepts them, and places them in the receipts, so far as I know. I do not know if this is a good criterion of comparative conscience: our financial system, for instance, is so close that fraud is difficult, and therefore occasions for restitution are rare. It seems to me that the number of restitutions might be used to show the probable number of frauds; and so perhaps an ingenious statistician might deduce from this that the country of most restitutions is that of the most fraud, and where the honesty of private persons is lowest, at least in their dealings with the State."

A German Professor replies: "I think that 'Conscience Money' is not paid in Germany, except in very rare cases. It is always reckoned among us as a characteristically English institution. On the whole there are certainly but very few frauds practised upon the State here, excepting small cases of frontier smuggling at the Customs. Such minor frauds appear to our middle classes as very venial sins, and do not trouble their conscience. And a man who practises large frauds is either a rogue, or acts from necessity; in neither case will he make restitution.

"To this it must be added that among you the preachers play a great part, and influence the mass of the people; this has not been the case with us now for a long time. Our Protestant Church is a Government Institution which has lost touch with the great mass of the people. When with you a preacher attacks unrighteous gains, the whole of the community which goes customarily to church every Sunday hears it. With us his sermon is heard by some old women and a couple of young girls confirmed the year before—certainly not people who have embezzled money."

As to these remarks we must note that there are far greater openings for getting an advantage over the State in England than there are on the Continent. The large amount raised as Income Tax—much of it on the unchecked voluntary declaration of the payer—is the main source of under-taxation; and the unfairness of the department has produced a state of public feeling which leads persons to avoid payments, who would not withhold them from other departments. Probate valuations are another source of under-payments—often honestly misstated at first, and corrected afterwards. And the general lack of official inspection of private life in England, and the liberty of the individual prevents the espionage which would readily intercept frauds in some other countries.

On the other hand, if opportunities of fraud are greater the inducements to restitution are also greater. The religious moral influence, noted by my German friend, undoubtedly counts for a good deal, especially as such an influence may lead to restitution while merely transitory. But still more, perhaps, the sense of fair play leads to honesty; this fairness is, perhaps, mainly due to the youthful training in competitive games, in which unfairness or oppression is reprobated; and it is seen perhaps most plainly in after life in the conduct of the English policeman, who is the servant of the public, and not the State regulator like the Continental official. Another reason for restitutions is strongly pointed to by the character of the payments. The postponing of sums under £5 until they amount to a £5 note shows that much of the payments are due from chronic under-taxation which accumulates. This points to this restitution not being made for intentional fraud, but by perfectly honest people; such may know that they are undertaxed but they prefer to pay up voluntarily rather than give information to the official taxgatherer; for that would lead him to worry and bully them in later years about the same sources, and require them to prove a diminutive of the income. It is far less inconvenient to pay up excess on an under-estimate than to have to pull down too high an estimate afterwards. More fair play on the part of the taxers would lead to more openness and honesty of the taxed.

NOTE D.

THE NATURE OF THE *KA*

AMONG the various attempts to understand what the Egyptians described as the *Ka*, little notice seems to have been taken of the examples afforded us in the Precepts of Ptah-hotep. They are the more valuable as being all of one age, and by one writer, so that they must represent and delimit a single conception, and their date is so early—in the Vth Dynasty—that they probably show the original idea.

In precept 7 the guest is enjoined not to pierce his host at table with many glances; "it is an abomination to the *ka* for them to be directed at him." Here the *ka* is the consciousness or self-consciousness of the man, annoyed by staring.

Then in precept 10, "Diminish not the time of following the heart (enjoying pleasures), for that is an abomination to the *ka* that its moment should be disregarded." The *ka*, therefore, is the seat of the intention and desire of enjoyment.

In precept 8, "The washing of the heart shall not be repeated (words said in passionate relief of the feelings), it is an abomination to the *ka*." Here the *ka* suffers the annoyance of another person's ill-temper.

In precept 12 a son who is mentally like his father is said to be "thy own son to whom it belongeth that thy *ka* begat." Here the *ka* comprises the mental qualities which were inherited, beyond the merely bodily form.

And the *ka* is the seat of generosity and kindness, for in precept 7 "it is the *ka* that openeth the hands" of the host;

and in precept 27 is mentioned the "master on whose *ka* depend thy provisions."

From all these instances we can fairly delimit the *ka* as being the inner mental consciousness and powers of thought, as apart from the influence of the senses and the communication with the body. The Egyptian argued, "If I burn myself it hurts the body, if I wash myself it cleanses the body. But there is something else inside which can have the analogous sensations to burning or to washing without anything being done to the body. This must be then an invisible being apart from the body; and as it has sensations and feelings of its own it must be like the body." Hence a second body of an immaterial kind was postulated as the image of the mind or inner consciousness. This will perfectly agree to the theory of the *ka* wandering about the cemetery after death and needing sustenance. And this accords with the powers and nature of the *ka* as shown in the tale of Setna, here discussed in the second lecture, where we concluded that "It has then all the full properties of mind, but not the abilities to act with force upon matter." There is little, if any, difference between this and what we define as the soul, except that it has a bodily — though immaterial — form.

PLYMOUTH
WILLIAM BRENDON AND SON
PRINTERS

www.ingramcontent.com/pod-product-compliance
Lightning Source LLC
Chambersburg PA
CBHW020254170426
43202CB00008B/368